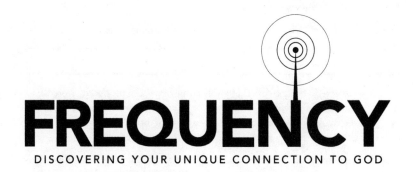

FREQUENCY

DISCOVERING YOUR UNIQUE CONNECTION TO GOD

ERIC PARKS + CASEY BANKORD

WORTHY
PUBLISHING

In memory of Bruce Boomsma,

You dreamed big dreams! Your natural optimism and strong faith led you to be involved in the big idea of Monvee. The kingdom of God will grow because of your response and faithfulness. Like you often said, "It's all good."

Contents

Contents

Foreword

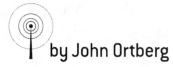

by John Ortberg

God made individuals.

God made you.

God had a reason.

Of course, God didn't make *only* you. God made lots of other people who matter just as much to Him. One of the great gods of our age is named Narcissus, who tries to convince each of us that we are the center of the universe. But perhaps the reason individualism can be such a dark problem when individuals have gone wrong is that individuals are so precious and good when they go right. God chose to create you. You can be sure He had very good reason for doing so. What He has in mind for your redemption will be glorious beyond all imagination. The point of this truth is not to feed a neurotic need for glory, but to recognize God is a glorious God who does not do inglorious things. Part of what this means is that you were created to have your relationship with God in a way that will not be replicated by any other person. C. S. Lewis writes this in *The Problem of Pain:* "[God] makes each soul unique. If He had no use for all these differences, I do not see why He should have created more souls than one. Be sure that the ins and outs of your individuality are no mystery to Him; and one day they will no longer be a mystery to you."[1]

C. S. Lewis was saying that we are all created to know and see God in a unique way, because we are all unique individuals. We are made to see a part of God in a way that nobody else might see it. When we realize that and praise God for it, we help other people come to see and know God better as well. And thus, we all enrich each other. Lewis explains, "If all experienced God in the same way and returned Him an identical worship, the song of the Church triumphant would have no symphony, it would be like an orchestra in which all the instruments played the same note."[2]

We all see God in a little different way. That's part of why we are created as individuals. Therefore, we are able to praise Him with a different note. And when all those notes come together, it is a symphony; it is a work of beauty that we are unable to grasp. The ability to perceive God, to be sensitive to His presence and leading, is a spiritual skill that can be learned. It is individual but also universal. It is why this book was written. It is the journey on which you now embark.

You were designed to play your own tiny but indispensable part in this symphony of cosmic beauty. No one else can sound your note. Your existence is integral to the goodness of the universe. It was created by God and designed by God to make a contribution that no one else can make. That is why it is a very good thing that you are who you are.

When you are most fully surrendered to God, you become most fully yourself. You can learn to attune your heart to God, for His sake, and the sake of all He made. That is what the idea of your frequency is about.

Now it is time to learn.

PART 1

YOUR FREQUENCY

chapter 1

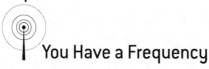

You Have a Frequency

There are moments in every person's life when all things just seem to make sense. In those moments, what you are doing or thinking matches perfectly with who you are and how you were made. It is a complete alignment and you think, *It doesn't get any better than this.* You want that moment to last and you want it more often. You have a sense of indescribable peace, feel an overwhelming sense of love, spontaneously laugh, or feel a rush of emotion.

If you thought hard enough about it, you probably would be able to identify at least one of those moments that felt like a place of completeness and satisfaction. It is in those moments, whether you realize it or not, that you experience God. You hit your frequency.

What Is Your Frequency?

In order to understand how your frequency with God works, it's helpful to understand how your body works. The human ear is amazing. The physiological process that happens in your ear, making it possible for you to hear, is complex and extraordinary. Every day our ears collect thousands of sound-wave frequencies that travel through a tiny path from the outer ear to a delicate organ in the inner ear called the cochlea.

Through the winding curves of your cochlea, there are millions of small cells attached to the basal membrane that extend tiny fingerlike projections into the fluid-filled cavity. These projections are called hair bundles. When sound waves or frequencies enter your ear, they move over these hairs—putting some into motion while others remain still. Each of these hairs has been programmed to detect a specific frequency—its favorite and only frequency. When it hears that frequency, the hair bundle bends and opens a small pore in the cell that allows a current to flow, sending the message to the brain. Out of thousands of frequencies that pass over that little hair bundle, it only knows and responds to the sound it was made to hear.

A dog barks, a friend calls your name, your phone rings, or a guitar strums. When you hear these sounds, millions of hair bundles, each tuned to their favorite frequency, are opening up, working together to make sense of it all, and then sending an organized message to your brain. It is intricate, specific, beautiful, and Godlike.

Genesis 1:27 says, "God created human beings in his own image" (NLT). What if God's ears work the same way ours do? Imagine the ear of God with millions of hair bundles tuned to specific frequencies—to specific lives. In the same way that God knows the number of hairs on your head, He knows your unique frequency. After all, He created it. He knows your voice and He listens to your life. He knows what is best for you and He knows when you are at your best. Job 12:10–11 says, "For the life of every living thing is in his hand, and the breath of every human being. The ear tests the words it hears just as the mouth distinguishes between foods" (NLT). God, in a way, has a hair bundle specifically for you.

MEETING GOD ON YOUR FREQUENCY

The Bible speaks about hearing throughout the Old and New Testaments,[1] inferring that there is something specific to be heard. In Exodus 15:26, God says to Moses, "If you listen carefully to the LORD your God and do what is right in his eyes, I will not bring on you any of the diseases I brought on the Egyptians." In the New Testament, the apostle Paul writes, "So then faith cometh by hearing, and hearing by the word of God" (Romans 12:16 KJV). God speaks to us in a variety of ways, but your God-given frequency is more than just sound. Living on your frequency is God's idea for ongoing connection with you. It's a way that you can live your whole life. He wants to walk with you, stir in you, and be available to you at all times. The Bible doesn't use the word *frequency* to describe connection with God, but the apostle Paul does refer to this type of connection in 1 Thessalonians 5:16–18 when he writes, "Rejoice always, pray continually, give thanks in all circumstances."

Over time, the concept of prayer as an ongoing conversation with God has often been replaced with certain postures of prayer such as kneeling, folding our hands, and closing our eyes. "Pray continually" gets interpreted as always being on your knees. Unfortunately, due to that misperception, much of what Paul was saying has been lost. And once that idea of ongoing connection with God was lost, it made our universal response to this verse, "That's just not possible."

How is it possible? You are not the only one asking. Charles Spurgeon, the renowned nineteenth-century preacher, once said, "It would be most unseemly, even if it were possible, for us to continue to unceasingly pray aloud. There would, of course, be no opportunity for preaching and hearing, for the exchange of friendly intercourse, for business, or for any other of the duties of life."[2] If we prayed all day, we would never have a chance to engage in conversation, exercise our faith, eat, or sleep! Praying out loud all day long or constantly kneeling is impossible for most people, but it is not impossible to have an ongoing connection with God where you can feel His presence, sense His voice, and stay on your frequency.

START IDENTIFYING

Think back to a moment when you felt connected to God, sensing His presence. Your moment, like your frequency, will be unique to you. It might have occurred in a beautiful natural setting where you experienced a moment of contemplative bliss. It might have been amid a frenzy of activity when you realized that you were doing exactly what you were designed to do. It might have been a moment of close personal connection with someone else or in a moment of quiet solitude. You can recall that instant when you thought, *It doesn't get any better than this.* Stop and reflect on your moment.

Where were you? Who was there? Can you remember what that felt like? Good. God intended for you to feel that. He created you to experience that moment of completeness in and through Him even if what you were doing seemed only vaguely spiritual. Make no mistake: He created this for you. That feeling or moment is exactly what happens when you intersect with your frequency. It's not a fluke, accident, or random stroke of luck. It is a powerful connection to the Spirit of God. And in that moment, you aren't the only one to notice.

LINDSAY'S STORY

Lindsay, a twenty-something artist, worked at a boutique design firm as a graphic designer and had recently decided to follow Jesus. She was excited and ready to serve. So when asked to be a group leader for a summer mission trip with one hundred high-school kids, she gladly accepted the opportunity.

The mission trip was in partnership with Safehouse Ministries in Atlanta, Georgia, and focused on providing physical labor and meal preparation at a new homeless shelter. Students were having a great time, and ministry progress was happening in a variety of ways. Then something unexpected happened and Lindsay found herself face-to-face with God.

Small groups of people had been going downtown to a park in the afternoons to casually get to know the "regulars." Lindsay volunteered to help keep the students in line one particularly sweltering day in June. When they got there, the students scattered throughout the park, but Lindsay was drawn to one small, undistinguished woman who was homeless. Lindsay later learned that the other homeless men and women in the park would not go near this particular woman because of her overwhelmingly pungent smell. Lindsay chose to ignore that.

Lindsay moved close to the woman, began to talk with her, and then hit her frequency. She sensed God saying, *Wash this woman's feet.* This is an example of those moments where you ask, "Really God? You want me to do *what?*" In a situation that would have normally been awkward, things became very clear to Lindsay. She was supposed to wash this woman's feet.

With gentle instruction and very few words, Lindsay asked the woman to sit on a park bench, and then she began to remove the woman's shoes. Lindsay had some Wet Wipes and hand sanitizer in her purse, so she pulled them out and began washing the woman's feet. People around the park stared with disbelief and astonishment. After all, they wouldn't go near her, but this young suburban professional was touching the untouchable. Her selfless action appropriately drew the attention of every person in the park. The woman seemed unsure and self-conscious at first, but she eventually felt comfortable enough to let Lindsay continue washing her feet.

Lindsay carefully cared for every corner of the woman's broken and tired feet. As Lindsay washed, she recognized that this was one of those *It doesn't get any better than this* moments. She could hear God and felt like He could hear her. As she cared for this woman, an unmistakable life filled that park.

Lindsay had hit her frequency, and everyone could sense it. The effects of that moment are still being felt to this day. Safehouse Ministries, inspired by the impact of Lindsay's simple act, does a "feet washing" day for the homeless in downtown Atlanta with every missions group that comes to serve.

POWER IN FREQUENCY

Frederick Buechner, theologian and author, writes, "The place God calls you to is the place where your deep gladness and the world's deep hunger meet."[3] When those two things meet, you experience God-infused power. When you hit your frequency, you feel an overwhelming sense of fulfillment that almost seems "otherly." And it is. God's supernatural power is in that moment. It is His power alive *in* you, the same power that brought Jesus back from the grave (Eph. 1:19–20). Living on your frequency is a powerful thing. It is a connection with a God who wants to do amazing things in and through your life to make an indelible impact on the world.

GROWTH IN FREQUENCY

When the Bible talks about connecting with the Spirit of God, a metaphor that is often used is water. Jesus said, "Let anyone who is thirsty come to me and drink" (John 7:37). Water is essential to life. Psalm 1:3 says that people who delight in God "are like trees planted along the riverbank, bearing fruit each season. Their leaves never wither, and they prosper in all they do" (NLT).

Water illustrates the redemptive power of God's presence as an always-moving river that sustains and refreshes. A tree's job is not to grow; it is to be planted along the riverbank. In order to survive and thrive and, most importantly, produce fruit, a tree has to have a life-giving connection to water. Like a tree connected to the river, you are designed to connect to God. If you stay connected with Him on your frequency and access the life in it, you will produce fruit. In the park that day, Lindsay connected with God, heard His voice, and responded, bearing visible fruit to those who were watching. There is unmistakable power and growth in a life that is living on its frequency.

Your ability to find your frequency and live on it has nothing to do with your bank account, your education, your job, your church, or how you grew up. None of these things prequalify or disqualify you. You are made with a frequency and you must recognize it, stay on it, and allow God to work through your life. Your frequency is not just a feeling. It is more than a mood. When you connect with it, the transforming power of God's Spirit will begin to work in your heart and, like in Lindsay's story, people's lives will be affected for the good, including your own.

Heart Change

Being on your frequency will change your heart too. Jesus is not primarily interested in improving how you look, how you feel, or even how others see you. God has a plan in mind, and He desires to redeem you. He is intent on transforming you in such a way that your life radiates the goodness and glory of God.

On your own, you can try to project an image and choose to make changes in your lifestyle. But making mere behavior modifications pales in comparison to what God truly wants to do in your life. An ongoing connection with God on your frequency will change your heart. Your heart is what God is after. "The LORD does not look at the things people look at. People look at the outward appearance, but the LORD looks at the heart" (1 Sam. 16:7).

God doesn't just want our compliance; He wants our heart. For better or for worse, we live from our heart. All we say and do—the good, the bad, and the ugly; both the private actions that make up our everyday lives and the very public actions of nations and governments—ultimately have their source in the human heart. Jesus said it this way: "A good man brings good things out of the good stored up in his heart, and an evil man brings evil things out of the evil stored up in his heart. For the mouth speaks what the heart is full of" (Luke 6:45).

That is why Jesus didn't come to change political, economic, or educational systems. His revolution to change the world was aimed squarely at changing human hearts. As hard as we might try, we can't change our hearts on our own, nor can we change others' hearts through clever convincing. God is the author of the kind of heart change we seek, and it is in your frequency where your personal transformation is found.

Just as He uniquely designed your hair, your eye color, and

your DNA, God thought up and intentionally designed your personality, strengths, weaknesses, and your pathway to Him. It is through His power alone that you are able to get the divine nudge you need to get your heart recalibrated, to get back to your original intent. And make no mistake: finding your frequency is not something you do once and move on. It is an ongoing, heart-on-heart connection with God.

FREQUENCY REQUIRES EFFORT

Dallas Willard, author of *The Spirit of the Disciplines,* said it this way: "You must act and you must act intelligently, for without intelligent action nothing happens. In effect, Jesus says, 'without me you can do nothing, but if you do nothing, it will be without me.'"[4] We have a role to play in the process of living on our frequency. It requires effort. We can't wait idly by and expect God to grow us without doing anything ourselves. We must do our part.

Imagine a sailor with a beautiful sailboat that is rigged with all the features it needs to sail—ropes, a harness, pulleys, and sails. The sailor can tie all the fancy knots, hoist every sail, and work from sunup until sundown; but ultimately, if the wind doesn't blow, the boat won't move.

On the other hand, the wind can howl with gale-force power; but if that same sailor doesn't come up from below deck to tie the fancy knots, hoist his sails, and do all that is necessary for the boat to set sail, then the boat won't move. As it relates to living on our frequency and allowing God to transform our hearts, we are the sailor and God's Spirit is the wind. He is the One who blows those winds of change our way, and it is our job to recognize when the Spirit is moving and then act.[5]

You must act and you must act intelligently. What do you do? What do you need to know about yourself to dial into your frequency? How do you find it? What types of things push you off your frequency?

I Can't Do It

Most people want to be changed for the better. Yet there seems to be a quiet seed of doubt that lies just beneath each person's veneer of hope. It whispers, "You can't do it! Some people can, but not you. You're too much like so-and-so; you always say the wrong thing at the wrong time; you are too dumb, too slow, too stubborn, too prideful, or too undisciplined to experience anything remotely close to what God has in mind for you. Face it, that kind of life is highly unlikely." Sadly, accepting these lies has become the norm for so many Christians, resulting in a tragically bored, unchanged, and uninspired life.

Many of us have settled for random encounters with God. A life where once in a while we accidentally encounter God on a retreat, vacation, mission trip, conversation, or through a worship song in a church service, and amazing things happen. In these all-too-rare moments, our lives intersect with our frequency and we get recalibrated, but then we struggle to stay there or find that type of moment again.

Look at it this way. . . .

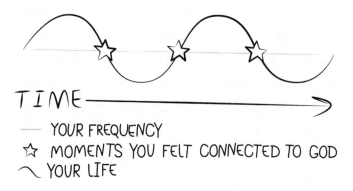

TIME ⟶
—— YOUR FREQUENCY
☆ MOMENTS YOU FELT CONNECTED TO GOD
⌒ YOUR LIFE

The curvy line is your life. The point at which the curvy line intersects the straight line resembles one of those significant moments where you say, "It doesn't get any better than this."

As you can see, most of your life is lived outside of a connection with God. Is that the abundant life that Jesus came to bring us? In John 7:38, Jesus said, "Whoever believes in me, as Scripture has said, rivers of living water will flow from within them." Are random moments with God what Jesus was really talking about when He talked about rivers of living water flowing through us? If we are to expect only random moments with God, it would be safe to assume that Jesus would say something more like, "I have come to give you a few good times" or "Random drops of living water will occasionally flow through you."

Jesus said that He came that we may have life and have it to the *full* (John 10:10). He wants us to have a life filled with regular moments of indescribable peace, indomitable power, and amazing grace. These are the moments when you meet Jesus and He forms you, shapes you, and gives you a renewed sense of His goodness and life-giving presence in your life. What if you could shorten the waves in your life and intersect your frequency with God more often? What if transformation is possible for the average, ordinary person?

James Hudson Taylor was an English missionary to China who founded the China Inland Mission, which at his death included 205 mission stations with over 800 missionaries and 125,000 Chinese Christians. He profoundly stated, "I have found that there are three stages in every great work of God: first, it is impossible, then it is difficult, then it is done."[6] Jesus said in Matthew 19:26, "With man this is impossible, but with God all things are possible." It is possible. You can do this. You can't produce transformation on your own, but get on your frequency, surrender to God's work in your life, and watch what happens.

Some Thoughts before Moving On

First, your frequency is not a formula that you can memorize and apply. It's a journey and lifelong process. God has put you on an adventure, and He wants to be with you the whole way. Your frequency is different from anyone else's, and it will require intentional effort to find it.

Second, because you have your own unique frequency, be careful how you listen to other people's advice. Their frequency is different from yours. Apply and seek wisdom; you would be a fool not to. But be careful not to blindly apply what other people are doing to stay on their frequency as the "silver bullet" for your life. The goal is to connect with God—on your frequency.

Third, finding your frequency cannot be outsourced. It's not your church's job, your spouse's job, your small group's job, or your mentor's job. It's your job. Community will help you along the way, but the responsibility is yours. We hope to provide you some helpful tools and ideas in this book for you to do that.

Now let's look at how you can find your frequency.

Chapter 2

Finding Your Frequency

No two people are the same. Stop and think about that for a second. There are approximately 6.84 billion people alive today.[1] Isn't it hard to believe that there isn't one person who looks exactly like another? And when you take personalities, traits, IQ, and DNA into account, the disparities grow even larger. There is not one person on the planet who has the same fingerprint as you.

In the same way, we are all different when it comes to how we find and tune into our God-given frequency. Understanding that uniqueness is at the center of what it takes for each of us to grow. John Ortberg, author of *The Me I Want to Be*, writes, "God never grows two people the same way. God had Abraham take a walk, Elijah take a nap, Joshua take a lap, and Adam take the rap. He gave Moses a forty-year time-out, gave David a harp and a dance, and gave Paul a pen and a scroll. He wrestled with Jacob, argued with Job, warned Cain, and comforted Hagar. He gave Aaron an altar, Miriam a song, Gideon a fleece, Peter a name, and Elisha a mantle."[2] As we discuss our frequency, your instinct may be to emulate someone you admire or who frequently connects with God on his or her frequency. You will see that strategy fail. Your frequency is yours; their frequency is theirs.

Often when pastors start describing their devotional practices from the pulpit, every person in the church begins to believe that they should do the exact same thing. People try it and it works for some, but for most of the congregation, it becomes frustrating. The same is true when it comes to spiritual leaders. You read or watch stories about Mother Teresa, C. S. Lewis, or Billy Graham and immediately think you need to start doing what they did and then expect to see the same results. You try it, it doesn't work, and you go back to feeling inadequate, incompetent, or unspiritual. At the risk of sounding redundant, you simply weren't meant to live on their frequency.

God will not ask why you didn't act more like your neighbor or best friend or spouse or Mother Teresa. He will not ask you why you didn't do things exactly the way your mentor did. He made you, He knows how you operate, and He knows the frequency He created you with—the way you were meant to connect with Him. When you try to live on someone else's frequency or try to connect with God in ways that are foreign to your unique wiring, you will be frustrated.

A lot of times, that frustration can lead you to the point of giving up completely, thinking that you are just not cut out for what it means to follow Jesus. You may disguise your frustration with busyness, indifference, opposition to faith, or expressing frustration with an unimportant issue, giving you permission to stay stuck or plateaued. When you try to live on someone else's frequency, it will feel like it doesn't fit. And it doesn't. It's not meant to. Try again, but this time, try it on your own frequency.

To be clear, this doesn't let you off the hook when it comes to discipline, sustained effort, and commitment. You'll need those things, even when you are on your frequency. However, you need to be cautious about trying to force yourself to be something or someone you are not.

FUEL FOR GROWTH

The fuel for growth is different for each of us. When you try to apply fuel for growth other than what you are wired to take, it doesn't work. Actually, it can be very destructive. Consider a plant and a lawn mower. They both need fuel to operate, but the liquid they each need is very different. A lawn mower needs gas to mow and a plant needs water to grow. Neither one can run without its respective fuel. But they cannot run on the other's fuel. Can you imagine people trying to green their grass by spraying gasoline all over it? Not safe. Worse yet, it would kill everything green in the process. And water would kill a lawn mower. It is the same with your frequency. Every person is not designed to run on the same type of fuel. One of the greatest challenges we face as Christians is the temptation to try to run our lives on someone else's fuel. Gary Thomas writes, "All too often, Christians who desire to be fed spiritually are given the same, generic, hopefully all-inclusive methods—usually some variation on a standardized quiet time. Why? Because it's simple, it's generic, and it's easy to hold people accountable to. But, for many Christians, it's just not enough."[3]

We live in a mass-production age and many of us have tried to do spiritual formation in our churches on a mass-production scale. A typical approach to spiritual growth in church is, "If we can get everyone to do the same stuff, read the same book, and join the same type of small group, then we will have done our job in helping our people grow." Really? Have everyone do the exact same thing? You don't have to look far to discover that these one-size-fits-all approaches to growth don't work with people who need different types of fuel. On the backside of those experiences, feelings of failure, inadequacy, and frustration become the norm.

THE WAY YOU ARE MADE

An understanding of the uniqueness of individuals is being applied in many areas in our culture. There are an ever-growing variety of personality assessments, as well as numerous books and seminars with the shared goal of helping people clearly understand how their skills and natural abilities apply to their job or education. In spite of this growing awareness of individuality, we have been slow to apply this same approach to how we grow spiritually and connect with God.

Malcolm Gladwell, author of the books *Tipping Point* and *Blink,* spoke at the TED conference in February 2004 about the significance of human variability. He referenced the work of Howard Moskowitz, a psychophysicist and research analyst. Howard specialized in consumer food analysis including products like coffee, mustard, and spaghetti sauce. According to Gladwell, over the last twenty-five years, there has been a movement in the food business away from discovering cooking universals (what everyone thinks would taste good) and a movement toward a deeper understanding of variability (what tastes good to each individual). Howard Moskowitz discovered, through a variety of experiments, that all people could be classified into specific clusters of taste preferences, as it pertains to certain foods. This discovery explains why we now have dozens of different styles of spaghetti sauce on the grocery store shelf (plain, spicy, chunky, extra chunky, traditional, garlic, etc.).

The idea of variability is important and relevant in every area of our life. And in most cases, if you were to ask people what they prefer, they don't exactly know. For example, Gladwell states that most people say they prefer a "dark, rich, hearty" roast of coffee, when in reality all they want is "milky, weak" coffee. Most of us don't know which kind of spaghetti sauce we like because we haven't tried them all. Often we think we prefer one thing when in actuality we prefer another. This is especially true in our spiritual lives. We may not know what we like, what works, what we should try, or what we should stop trying. Therefore, we end up lost and confused as we stand in front of the grocery store shelf of spiritual choices, so to speak.[4]

When asked about the impact an individual's personality has on spiritual growth, John Ortberg said,

> You are God's handiwork. The Psalmist says, "For we know He has made us and not we ourselves." Now, on the one hand, that is very humbling because that means I am not a self-made person, I did not create myself, and I cannot take credit for stuff that I do. And, on the other hand, it is staggering because if I am very serious about the fact that God made me, then I have to ask myself, "What kind of engineer do I think God is? Is it likely that God would have left out parts that should have been included or made an error when creating me?"[5]

Have you ever asked God why He didn't make you more like someone else? Most of us have. It's easy to believe that God made someone else superior to you—he or she is a masterpiece and you are a mistake. That is false. Scripture is clear that to be created by God is to be made in His image and created without defect in His eyes.

In order to experience regular moments with God on your frequency and transformational growth, you must take into account the way you are constructed. There are constants when it comes to following God. Disciplines like prayer, service, attention to Scripture, and participation in authentic community are essential for every Christ-follower. But the simple truth is that not every person who is trying to follow Jesus has to do those things in the exact same way. As it relates to your frequency, it is wise to consider the specific attention God pays to every element of the way you were created.

In order for you to intentionally live on your frequency, you must understand your spiritual pathway, learning style, and various personality traits. They are clusters of preferences that will help you navigate the wide variety of choices you choose from every day. They are important to experiencing the life God intended for you and pivotal to experience sustainable, life-changing spiritual growth. As you review the descriptions below, start thinking about the way you most naturally connect with God and how it applies to your frequency.

SPIRITUAL PATHWAYS

One of the things that makes us different in our frequencies is known as "spiritual pathways." A number of respected authors, including Gary Thomas, Bill Hybels, and Ruth Haley Barton, have explored this topic in greater detail.[6] Basically, the consensus is that spiritual pathways are the avenues and/or environments where you most easily and effortlessly connect with God. Different authors have had different lists and labels for each pathway, but here are seven pathways to consider as you attempt to identify this very important component of your frequency.

Activist Pathway

People on the activist pathway experience God through activities that require a high level of energy and passion for action.

People on the activist pathway love challenges and opposition. They love a fast-paced, problem-filled, complex, and strenuous way of life. They love to do things for God. These types want to run hard and they are energized by it. They are hardwired to look for and depend on God's presence and guidance in the heat of battle. They need causes. It doesn't have to be glamorous or visible, but it has to demand the best they have to offer. Without that, their spiritual life will stagnate.

Contemplative Pathway

People on the contemplative pathway experience God most when they have time to think deeply without distraction.

People on the contemplative pathway love large blocks of

uninterrupted time alone. Reflection and observation come naturally to them. Images, metaphors, and simple thoughts help them as they pray. They have a large interior world of intrapersonal communication, and they don't require much external stimulation. Making time to listen to God in silence and solitude is vital to the health of their souls and necessary for them to experience a deepening sense of God's presence. They need regular, protected, intense, and undistracted times alone.

Creation Pathway

People on the creation pathway experience God most when they are in or around nature.

People on the creation pathway are energized and replenished by being outdoors. They love camping, fishing, golfing, boating, or any activity that requires interaction with nature. If they are cooped up inside for too long, their soul starts to feel stale and uninspired. They see God in the spectacular, but also in the everyday outside world. People on this pathway need to spend large chunks of time outdoors. When they do, they will begin to sense a growing desire for God.

Intellectual Pathway

People on the intellectual pathway experience God the most when they are challenged intellectually and they are learning more about Him.

People on the intellectual pathway are energized by intellectually stimulating conversations and debates. Ideas are as alive to them as people are to others. They love to study Scripture. They love thinking about theology. They read a lot. When in church, they usually don't enjoy the creative or music portion of the service nearly as much as the message. They solve problems by analysis and logic. They feel closest to God when learning about Him through great books, deep thoughts, complex conversations, and sound teaching.

Relational Pathway

People on the relational pathway experience God the most when they are involved in significant relationships.

People on the relational pathway consider their close friends and community experiences to be indispensable. For the most part, being alone drives them crazy. They rarely meet a stranger. Often people with a relational pathway experience key spiritual moments—being convicted of sin, or encouraged to persevere—as God speaks to them through other people. They hear God speak to them more in a conversation than from a book.

Serving Pathway

People on the serving pathway experience God most tangibly when they are actively helping others.

People on the serving pathway love to serve. They grow

spiritually when they make observations about themselves or God when they are serving. Often they will have an epiphany, spiritual thought, or special moment of sensing God's presence when meeting the needs of another person. They feel alive and connected to God more by doing than by thinking.

Worship Pathway

People on the worship pathway experience God the most in moments of worship.

People on the worship pathway have a natural gift for expression and celebration. Something deep inside of them feels released when they are able to voice their praise and adoration for God. Some of their most formative moments occur during times of musical worship. They need to experience great worship on a regular basis. Likely, these types of people have favorite songs they listen to over and over as a way to connect with God.

LEARNING STYLES

Discovering your learning style is another important component to finding your frequency. Any good teacher knows that every student connects the dots differently. So do you. By understanding how you process information and learn, you will be able to discern what elements and practices will put you closer or further from your frequency. Learning styles have been studied, written about, and discussed for decades. Here are five primary learning styles.[7]

Auditory Style

If you learn best by listening, you may like to work while listening to sound and/or music. You notice the music playing in the background of movies, TV shows, and other media. You often find yourself humming or tapping a song or jingle. In a classroom or seminar, you find yourself concentrating on what the speaker is saying rather than copiously taking notes. You remember important phrases, lyrics from songs, or lines from movies better than others.

Classroom Style

If you learn best in a classroom, you most likely enjoy more than one style of learning. The combination of auditory, visual, and discussion benefits you more than others. While this is not a traditional learning style, it represents how many of us have become comfortable learning. You learn best when physically engaged in a hands-on activity in the company of other people. Taking tests and measurably tracking your progress is energizing to you. You like checklists and getting things done.

Social Style

If you learn best socially, you communicate well with people verbally and nonverbally. You typically prefer learning in groups or classes, or you like to spend one-on-one time with a teacher or an instructor. You heighten your learning by bouncing your thoughts off other people and listening to how they respond. You prefer to work through issues, ideas, and problems with a group. You thoroughly enjoy working with a synergistic group of people. You like to stay around after class and talk with others. You prefer social activities, rather than doing your own thing.

Verbal Style

If you learn best verbally, you love to write, read, and talk. It is easier for you to remember information once you have written it down or explained it to someone else. When you are trying to remember something or recall a conversation, you will catch yourself saying it out loud to yourself. You know the meaning of many words and regularly make an effort to find the meaning of new words. You use these words, as well as phrases you have picked up recently, when talking to others.

Visual Style

If you learn best by watching, you remember new information best through images and pictures. You can easily visualize objects, plans, and outcomes in the way you remember them looking. You also have a good spatial sense, which gives you a good sense of direction. You can easily find your way around using maps and rarely get lost if you can visualize where you are going. When taking a test or committing something to memory, you often remember how the text or graph looked on the page. You enjoy taking notes or using a whiteboard to explain an idea.

Your Personality

Each element of your personality plays an important role in your relationship with God. There are things that will come more naturally to you, and things that won't. Certain types of spiritual practices will energize the way you think and others won't. Understanding your personality as it pertains to your frequency is just as, if not more, important as your learning style and pathway to God.

Assessing personality styles has also become more common. There are a variety of personality assessments available today to help you determine your strengths, weaknesses, passions, and skill set. This is a good thing. The more we understand about others and ourselves, the better we can interact with the world around us.

An ancient personality profile called the Enneagram has been used by many people throughout history.[8] Historians debate how it actually originated, but it is a simple, clear, and relevant approach to how you can apply your personality to finding and living on your frequency. According to the research and scholarship around the Enneagram, there are nine basic types of personalities, with variations. As you read through the descriptions, start thinking about which one you are and how it applies to your frequency.

The Reformer

The reformer is disciplined, strong, responsible, wise, and organized. People with this type of personality are able to overcome adversity and have a strong moral compass. They work hard to be seen as a person who is honest and full of integrity. They love checklists, clear communication, and situations where there are clear right and wrong answers. As a self-proclaimed perfectionist, this type of person can easily become judgmental and relationally cold if they are not careful.

The Helper

The helper is altruistic, generous, enthusiastic, thoughtful, and sympathetic. People with this type of personality are usually great listeners, caring, and dependable. They value the details of each person's life and they love to help people when they need it. They are nurturing, encouraging, and genuinely interested in the lives of others. Because these types of people enjoy helping others, they have a hard time saying no when they need to and often care too much about what people think of them.

The Achiever

The achiever is driven, charismatic, industrious, confident, and energetic. People with this type of personality are usually born leaders and winsome with others. They are contagious to be around, and most people want to be a part of the things they do. They like to develop their skills and abilities in order to be successful. Because these types of people are driven and ambitious, they tend to mask their inadequacies and try too hard for the applause of people.

The Individualist

The individualist is imaginative, honest, profound, inquisitive, and passionate. People with this type of personality feel things deeply and are abundantly creative. They have an uncanny ability to turn something ordinary into something extraordinarily beautiful. They are able to see the positive side to most difficult situations. Because these people feel things deeply, they have the tendency to hold grudges and harness negative feelings for too long if they are not careful.

The Investigator

The investigator is intelligent, witty, independent, mysterious, and sensible. People with this type of personality are observant, understanding of the details, and solution-oriented. They are able to analyze a large amount of information with great proficiency and develop clear explanations for complex things. Because these people pride themselves on thinking logically and systematically, they can become very insecure when they don't know the answer to a dilemma and feel cornered with no way out.

The Loyalist

The loyalist is authentic, dependable, sacrificial, warm, and discerning. People with this type of personality are committed to a cause and stand up for what they feel is right. They are hardworking and do what they say they are going to do. They are willing to go to great lengths to accomplish a mission. Because these people have an enormous sense of responsibility, they can be plagued with a sense of not doing enough and worry about outcomes they cannot control.

The Enthusiast

The enthusiast is playful, optimistic, versatile, resilient, and curious. People with this type of personality are willing to try anything and usually have fun doing it. They are multitalented, involved in a variety of things, and consider themselves to be fast learners. To them, there is nothing like an adventure. While the joy of new experiences is blossoming in this type of person, they can become overcommitted, overstimulated, and terribly afraid of becoming bored.

The Challenger

The challenger is dynamic, resourceful, self-confident, persistent, and decisive. People with this type of personality are rarely intimidated and are inspiring to follow. They love taking charge of the situation and helping those who cannot help themselves. They love providing opportunities for other people to thrive. They have a strong work ethic and a higher energy level than most people, but it can approach a danger zone when they set unrealistic expectations on themselves and others and don't care properly for their heart, body, and soul.

The Peacemaker

The peacemaker is patient, unpretentious, good-natured, open minded, and kind. People with this type of personality are excellent mediators and promoters of healthy community. They know how to keep the peace among family, friends, and coworkers. They are naturally drawn to spiritual things and have a strong desire for a deep connection with God. Because of their commitment to peace and harmony, they can be resistant to tough conversations and the resolving of conflict, which leads them to be disengaged and passive.

SAME DESTINATION, DIFFERENT PATH

While we all take different paths, the destination is the same—an encounter with God. Your spiritual pathway, learning style, and personality are important to consider as you pursue your frequency. That being said, God is always available to you. People have connected with God for centuries without knowing their specific pathway, learning style, or personality. Unfortunately, many of us have lived for far too long not knowing and not succeeding and, therefore, not trying. Every life is important and no one should get to take a pass on growth. You are destined to know God deeply and be transformed every day because of it.

Some Thoughts before Moving On

Your uniqueness is a gift from God, not a reason to feel entitled. The danger in talking about uniqueness is that it allows room for someone to say, "Well, [insert any spiritual discipline] doesn't work for me; therefore, I'm not going to do it." Please understand—that is not what we are saying. Your unique wiring is a reality that you must consider in order to predictably and regularly connect with God on your frequency. There is a goal for each of us to actively pursue—a growing relationship with Jesus.

Living on your frequency is also not a reason to be disrespectful to authority. Your pastor or mentors have been tasked to do their absolute best to guide you onto the right path for growth. Their teaching, recommendations, and life examples matter and you should pay attention to them. Yes, you may not be wired like them and your path will likely look different. But be respectful and honoring to those in leadership.

Community and an appropriate amount of authority are always better than isolation.

The Bible, prayer, service, and authentic Christian community are essential to every person regardless of his or her pathway, learning style, or personality. Figure out how these core components of faith fit into your frequency and value them. They are the source of immeasurable truth and a catalyst to sustainable growth.

Now let's find out what is getting in the way of you finding your frequency.

Chapter 3

Something Is in the Way

The biggest barrier to living the life God intended for us is simple—it is sin. Sin is a powerful force that expresses itself in our lives in different ways and in different forms. It looks more or less tempting at different times, but the results are the same. And in most cases, our sin is closely related to our strengths. Because we are unique, we each have unique habits of sin (correlating to our personality) that tend to get in the way of our growth and cause us to live outside our frequency.

Frequency Blockers

If sin is the most disruptive force to your frequency, then how do you—in cooperation with the Holy Spirit—move past it? The apostle Paul laid the groundwork for how to deal with this dilemma when he wrote, "Throw off your old sinful nature and your former way of life. . . . Instead, let the Spirit renew your thoughts and attitudes. Put on your new nature, created to be like God—truly righteous and holy" (Eph. 4:22–24 NLT).

There are two other passages, one in Colossians 3 and the other in Galatians 5, where Paul uses language that is similar to Ephesians 4 and the idea of "throwing off" sinful patterns of behavior. If you took these three passages and picked out the various things Paul listed as behaviors to throw off, you would see a remarkable list of bad, bad things. We, as humans, are capable of all kinds of evil when we are at our worst.

Paul didn't just show us the evil of which we are capable. In these sections of Scripture, he also laid out a separate set of ideals that we, as followers of Jesus, should be pursuing. We have come to know them as the fruit of the Spirit: love, joy, peace, forbearance, kindness, goodness, faithfulness, gentleness and self-control (Gal. 5:22–23). So the obvious question is, how do we put off the bad things and put on the good things? The answer: you can't! At least, you can't on your own. That is why they are called fruit *of the Spirit*. Many of us try to fake it, but it always eventually leads to frustration and emptiness. Remember the tree planted by the river in Psalm 1:3? The only path to fruit in our lives and the absence of evil is our life-giving connection with God—our frequency.

It's Like a Teeter-Totter

If you are a visual learner, the following illustration should make absolute sense. If you are not, you'll need to stretch yourself a little. We already pandered to the human anatomy types (with the "hair bundles") and the lawn-care amateurs with their lawn mower and grass. This one is for the engineers!

A teeter-totter is a staple at most children's playgrounds. With a long plank extending across a central stationary fixture, a teeter-totter allows kids to sit on either end, teetering and tottering up and down. Engineers know teeter-totters as class 1 levers. The function of teeter-totters, or class 1 levers, is built on three core elements that are crucial to understand as it applies to your frequency.

Inverse Relationship

First, there is a direct inverse relationship between what happens on each side of the teeter-totter. For example, if a toddler sits on one end of a teeter-totter and a sumo wrestler sits on the other end, what do you think will happen? The toddler better grow wings! A greater presence of an object on one end inversely affects what happens to the object on the other side. They are inextricably connected.

It works the same when it comes to the relationship between sin and the fruit of the Spirit in our lives—those character traits that the apostle Paul said we should allow the Spirit to put on us. This inverse relationship is key to understanding the process of how we can deal with sin. In Galatians, Colossians, and Ephesians, it is almost as if Paul is saying, "On the one hand, you have all this stuff to put off. And on the other hand, there is all this stuff to put on." The good things and the bad things don't belong together, but, like a teeter-totter, they directly affect each other. There is an inverse relationship between the bad and the good in your life. They are connected like the toddler and the sumo wrestler.

A greater presence of sin directly affects your ability to connect to your frequency and experience the fruit of the Spirit in your life. Take envy for example. Imagine a huge amount of envy on one end of the teeter-totter and a small amount of peace and joy on the other end. Which reality wins in your life? Envy.

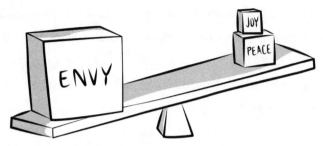

It is impossible for you to be peaceful and joyful when you are consumed with envy—no matter how hard you try to manufacture it. This is true for every core sin pattern we have, which is why we must pay special attention to the habitual sins in our lives that keep us stuck. Living life on our frequency is impossible and will be a fruitless pursuit if we are not willing to admit our sin and address it.

Grounded Principle

The second important concept to understand about teeter-totters is the grounded principle. In terms of the inverse relationship between "put off" and "put on," if something is grounded, it can become rooted. Whatever is rooted in your life is what feels real. By the very nature of the inverse relationship, if one side (the sumo wrestler) is grounded, then by definition of a class 1 lever, the other side (toddler) cannot be.

Have you ever struggled with a negative pattern in your

life—for example, prolonged anxiety or fear? If you have, then you understand the truth of this teeter-totter principle. If anxiety is dominant in your life, then it is grounded. If it is grounded then it becomes rooted, which makes the inversely related fruit of peace and joy unattainable (or up in the clouds somewhere with the toddler). It feels like the path to peace and joy is unrealistic, if not impossible.

The Fulcrum

There is a way to use the physics of a teeter-totter to your advantage. It has to do with the fulcrum. The fulcrum is the stationary piece in the middle of the teeter-totter. Engineers will tell you that if you move the fulcrum closer to the sumo, the toddler now has the advantage of leverage.

The Egyptians must have loved teeter-totters (or class 1 levers). They desperately needed them when they built the pyramids. How do you suppose they lifted extremely large rocks to use for construction? A class 1 lever has the fulcrum positioned strategically between the force and the load. With the fulcrum closer to the load (the sumo in our example), it is possible to gain a significant mechanical advantage. This advantage has been used throughout time to do what might not be possible without a class 1 lever. With this rule of physics, it became entirely possible for someone to use leverage to lift a weight far heavier than they could lift were they using their own strength alone.

The secret of the class 1 lever is not about your effort or your strength. The secret is the third concept you need to know about a teeter-totter: the power is in the fulcrum. By moving the fulcrum toward what is grounded, you can lift it. It doesn't matter how heavy the object is or how deep the roots are.

So if God's plan is for you to be changed, and you have a role in doing so, it's pretty clear what Paul was saying: move that fulcrum toward what is most grounded in your life and you will be able to uproot it. He urges us to have the uncompromising courage to identify the thing that is inhibiting the life Jesus has planned for us and to consistently put it off.

THE FULCRUM OF GOD'S TRUTH

Right in the middle of Paul's "throw off" and "put on" statements, there is a critical phrase that will help you understand how important the fulcrum is to our transformation. Paul says, "Let the Spirit renew your thoughts and attitudes" (Eph. 4:23 NLT). God is after heart change, but in order for that to happen, there needs to be a mind change. When a certain sin pattern has become rooted in our lives, we start to think things like, *It's really not that big of a deal* or *I can quit anytime* or *This is just for a season* or *This is what makes me happy.* Somewhere along the way, we are betrayed by our minds. And the only way to combat those lies we've started believing is to confront them with the truth.

Think of it this way: our fulcrum is the truth that God has given us. And like a teeter-totter, the closer the fulcrum (or truth) gets to the largest sin pattern in your life, the more you will able to lift it. The fulcrum is the point of equilibrium, the balancing point, where the work of God's grace, truth, and our surrender come together in one marvelous action of redemption.

When we are not afraid to honestly look at our life and face that which is keeping us from being all that God wants us to be, God shines a light on all the stuff that is grounded in our life. We come to Him praying like David prayed, "Search me, God, and know my heart; test me and know my anxious thoughts. See if there is any offensive way in me, and lead me in the way everlasting" (Ps. 139:23–24). God knows us better than we know ourselves. When we realize God is God and we are not, He can show us the whole truth, pointing out whatever is getting in the way.

Imagine what would happen if, in moments throughout our day, we took some practical steps to put off those spiritual inhibitors by believing what God says about us and then moving that truth toward our brokenness. If insecurity is what is rooted in me because of my struggle with envy, I must have the humility to admit it, recognize the lies I've believed, and begin to allow the Spirit of God to renew my mind and change my heart. When we do this, our sin becomes uprooted and the teeter-totter starts tipping toward the fruit of the Spirit. We don't have to work harder or become stronger; we just have to recognize where we are vulnerable, turn our attention there, and work in cooperation with God's power to uproot that reality in our life. As Paul wrote, "'My grace is all you need. My power works best in weakness.' So now I am glad to boast about my weaknesses, so that the power of Christ can work through me" (2 Cor. 12:9 NLT).

So does it work? Well, as with any analogy, the teeter-totter image is certainly imperfect. But at its core, there is a truth that has the potential to answer one major question we have about our role in God's process for us to grow: what do we do about sin that seems impossible to lift?

JEFF'S STORY

Jeff and his new bride, Ellen, had moved from the Midwest to picture-perfect Laguna Beach to accept a position as a youth pastor. But within a few short months, it became clear that this position was a less-than-perfect fit. Jeff and Ellen made enormous sacrifices to relocate to the West Coast in order to pursue what was so clear to them both—God's will. Blame it on unclear expectations or on youthful naïveté—either way, Jeff and Ellen saw the writing on the wall as the dream job slowly slipped from their grasp. Almost as soon as it had begun, it was over.

The landscape for this couple was seismically shifting. On the heels of their decision to leave the congregation they were serving, Ellen found out she was pregnant. But their joy amid the insecurity of a job change was short-lived. They miscarried.

"That was a very turbulent time for us," Jeff recalled, "as it is for any family. But for us it was particularly difficult because of everything else that led up to it. We had moved to Southern California, we were away from our families, and we went to work at the church, but that didn't work out the way we expected. Our faith was shifting, growing, changing, and evolving. Our spiritual lives and our everyday lives were not connecting. And Ellen and I were really drifting apart."

The confusion of their vocational disappointment, the pressure of finding a new job, and their lack of connections in the Orange County area led to a sense of isolation for both Jeff and Ellen. Their time in Laguna Beach took a major toll on their newly minted marriage.

"There is a part of me that felt like the baby was an attempt to save our relationship," Jeff said. "So when we miscarried, there was not only a sense of loss for our child, but loss for our marriage as well. Ellen was mad at God. She was mad at me, and things began to change."

Jeff and Ellen began to drift farther apart. "She just grew indifferent to being married and started building a whole new life apart from 'us.' I had no clue what she was up to most of the time. I watched her drift and eventually live like I wasn't there. I didn't really say much, thinking it would pass. We had made plans to go on a short vacation with another couple. Ellen didn't want to go, so I decided to go without her to give her space. I thought it might help. What is the old saying— 'Absence makes the heart grow fonder'? But it did the opposite for us and sealed the deal. By the time I got back, she had moved out of our bedroom into the spare room. I tried to figure out how to fix our marriage, but to no avail."

In less than a month after that fateful trip to the countryside, Ellen and Jeff—this couple who had pledged to always be together—put their house on the market, sold it, and became two single people living on their own.

"I met with her a couple of times and tried to convince her we needed to go to counseling together. I told her we should try to get back together because I just felt it wasn't right; we needed to work this out. But she treated our divorce like a high-school breakup—and she was always trying to get me to agree we should get divorced. But I didn't want that," Jeff lamented. "It didn't even feel real; it was like I was walking in a dream. I felt utterly lost."

Jeff said, "I remember thinking, *We are really going to get divorced. What are people going to think of me?* I was a pastor, and I felt called to ministry. I could never do that again. I didn't have a career, I didn't have a wife, and I didn't have a house. I didn't have anything. If I went back home, people would be talking about me. My life seemed over."

As Jeff described this moment, it was evident that the tee-ter-totter in Jeff's life in that season had swung toward all that would keep him down—toward bitterness, pain, and fear. He could feel it too, reliving that time, as he said, "My life seemed over."

Jeff remembered the point at which he knew it was over with Ellen. It was in that moment that bitterness became grounded in Jeff's life. Because of the inverse connection to joy, kindness, and forgiveness, those three things swung off the ground and into the air, becoming no longer real in his life. And Jeff didn't even know. By putting on bitterness and letting it become grounded in his life, he was at the same time putting off joy, kindness, and forgiveness—the very things he so desperately needed and wanted. He was drifting to a place where living on his frequency seemed utterly impossible.

Jeff said, "I had hit bottom and my spirituality was gone. I blamed God for the whole mess. I felt like He had snatched the rug from beneath my feet and I was still falling, tumbling, and spiraling out of control. In that moment, I told Him, 'I'm done with You.'"

Jeff still wanted to connect with God; he just did it through yelling. "I tried to tell God He didn't exist. It was funny—I made sure to address God when I told Him that He didn't exist. But there were distinct times when I could feel God whisper back, 'You know too much about Me, Jeff.'"

Jeff went on to explain how real the bitterness became in his life. He struggled to find a place of peace and some sort of joy, but it seemed impossible. He was always faking it. He grew cold inside and the longer bitterness stayed embedded in his heart, the darker life grew. After a while, Jeff began to realize that if he was ever going to rebuild his life, he needed to remove the thing that was blocking his frequency: bitterness. He needed to start with God, then with the church that had hurt him, and then, most importantly, his ex-wife.

"It took time, but eventually I began to make some decisions about my life, my future, and my ability to forgive. I quit pretending that I was okay and just got comfortable with the fact I wasn't okay." Jeff figured out he couldn't fake happiness and he couldn't just think happy thoughts. He needed to move his fulcrum (the truth) toward the thing that was in the way of a new life—bitterness.

Jeff began to let the Spirit change his mind and then eventually his heart. He recalled, "I remember starting by just picking up a few books and tapes. I grabbed *The Purpose Driven Life*[1] and read it cover to cover. I became really open about my brokenness and my troubled spirituality. I also had to deal with my bitterness toward my ex-wife. I began asking for forgiveness. I asked God. I asked those around me. If I felt I had wronged someone, I asked him or her for forgiveness. And it was crazy; I started feeling the power to forgive."

Jeff knew that the final step toward uprooting the bitterness in his life was to sit down with his ex-wife and forgive her. Mike Breaux, author of the book *Identity Theft*, describes forgiveness as "giving up your right to get even, and trusting the justice of God as you lean into his mercy and grace."[1] Ellen agreed to meet with Jeff.

"We met in a restaurant to sign the divorce papers. I felt like God asked me to tell her I forgave her. I sensed Him saying, 'Regardless of what she says or does, you need to forgive her.' So I signed the papers, gave them back to her, and then said, 'I want you to know that this was very painful, but I forgive you.' She didn't say a word, but I could feel a release—I felt some peace."

Uproot Your Frequency Blockers

Removing what is blocking your frequency means you are able to think, move, and act in ways that you otherwise could not. You are able to sense the presence of God—giving you confidence to do what you once thought was impossible. As Jeff continued to get back to living on his frequency and humbly recognized his natural tendency to block God's redemptive power in his life, he began to live in God's power.

Day by day, Jeff's practical steps to admit his sin and believe God allowed him to expose his sin with the truth of God. And over time, the full weight of joy, kindness, and even forgiveness swung toward the ground and crashed into Jeff's heart, embedding itself deep within his soul. In Jeff's case, the bitterness that had seemed almost inescapable floated to the margins of Jeff's life. That is the power of the teeter-totter. And that is the power available to you if you turn your attention toward what is blocking your frequency and trust God to help you uproot it in your life.

It Really Does Matter

Frequency connection happens. Every single day, people are becoming more of what they were made to be. While the process is different for each of us, the outcome remains the same—reclaiming the life Jesus had in mind for us.

Our task in putting off the sin that blocks our frequency

is simply to direct our attention toward the things we want to put off, recognize them, exchange lies for the truth, and surrender to God's power to uproot sin from our lives. Although at times it may feel that the putting off is impossible, when we surrender to God, move the fulcrum, and partner with the work of His Spirit in our lives, we find that it is possible. It is His grace that helps us become grounded in the fruit of the Spirit, not the fruit of ourselves.

You may have destructive habits in your life that are prevalent and that are blocking the way of change in your life. If you have a weakness that is weighing you down or you are spiritually stuck and don't know why, then you are in good company. You are in a great place to begin to see change. Remember that Jesus told Paul, "My grace is all you need. My power works best in weakness" (2 Cor. 12:9 NLT).

A MAN AND A LIZARD

There is a vivid scene in C. S. Lewis's book *The Great Divorce* where Lewis describes a man who has a lizard on his shoulder, representing the man's struggle with lust. An angel appears to the man and offers to kill the lizard. The man doesn't know if he wants that to happen because the lizard had whispered to the man, "Now, be careful; if you let him kill me, you will die too. There will be nothing left of you." The man comes up with all kinds of excuses: "I'm sure he will be quiet now. He is quite tame. I have him under control." But the angel says, "No, you must decide and it must die."

The man, overwhelmed by this decision, finally says, "Go ahead and kill it. God help me." Deep down he believes that if the lizard dies, he will die too.

The angel puts his hand around the lizard and chokes it to death. The man collapses to the ground in tremendous pain, expecting imminent death. But soon, he gets back up. Now he is different than before, shining like a god. The lizard comes back to life too, but now is a magnificent stallion. The lust had been transformed into a godly desire. This newly transformed man mounts the horse and soars into paradise.[3]

Lewis illustrates the importance of putting off the things that block our frequency and not believing the lies we all hear about our sin. Does that mean that everyone gets to go to paradise on a horse? Maybe not, but it does mean that the death of what is blocking life on your frequency allows the possibility of complete transformation.

Not What You'd Hoped

We live in a day where people really like the idea of being connected spiritually. So this idea of tapping into your frequency may seem attractive to many people because they want to be in touch with more power and energy. However, when spirituality becomes intrusive, it tends to become less attractive.

We want to be spiritual people if it means being more successful, more courageous, and having more peace. We would like a little self-improvement, but not total transformation. We say, "Well, yeah, but then I have to put off my selfishness and greed? I'm not so sure about that. Then I have to put off the bitterness I have toward my parents? I'm not so sure about that." In such moments, it seems much easier to live life without trying.

It is difficult work and you will need God's help to do it. Thankfully, you don't have to use your own strength to try to be more joyful, loving, and peaceful. Trust in God, move the fulcrum toward what is blocking your frequency, and watch what happens. The teeter-totter might just tip the other way toward real freedom.

SOME THOUGHTS BEFORE MOVING ON

This idea of uprooting our frequency blockers is countercultural to what is becoming a strengths-based culture. Marcus Buckingham in the book *Now, Discover Your Strengths* has championed the phrase, "Focus on your strengths and manage around your weaknesses."[4] This is true and extremely helpful in most contexts. We would wholeheartedly agree with this philosophy as it pertains to your learning style and spiritual pathway, as is evident with the previous chapter.

However, it's not entirely helpful when it comes to the issue of sin in the lives of Christians. For too many years, we have ignored or managed around the issue of sin in our lives while trying to focus mostly on our own effort to act better, put on a happy face, and artificially manufacture the fruit of the Spirit in our lives. It is exhausting, fruitless, and won't work. It hasn't worked. Sin is an issue that Scripture is clear about. Sin must be paid attention to, surrendered to God, and be lifted from our life by God's power. If not, it has the potential to get the best of us, blocking our ability to live life on our frequency and to know God the way He intended for us to know Him.

Grace is abundant and you'll need more than one chance at this. It's a lifelong process of trial and error, and we have a loving heavenly Father who picks us up when we fall. When you can intentionally address the primary frequency blocker in your life in ways that fit your learning style, pathway to God, and personality, you will be able achieve a level of precision and real growth that would otherwise not be possible.

Now let's look at the best way to craft a plan and get after it.

Chapter 4

Crafting a Plan

You have what it takes to grow. God has given you everything you need. He's created you uniquely and has given you a frequency. However, most of us wander through our life without a clear plan to live on that frequency. We are unaware of the things that keep us from connecting to God. We occasionally connect with God, but we don't have the faintest idea how to replicate that experience. As a result, we tend to settle into a day-to-day life that is devoid of the miraculous. It doesn't have to be that way. It shouldn't be that way. God didn't make you that way. His plan for your future is intended to be far beyond your imagination, but you must ask, "What is my part in that plan?"

THE JOYS OF PLANNING

The idea of planning has always been attractive to people who want to change. We've all experienced those moments where we've felt inspired to sit down, figure it all out, and then get after the plan we put in place. As it pertains to workouts, devotional practices, diets, etc., we stick to our plan for forty-eight hours, a few weeks, or maybe a couple of months, and then we get too busy, tired, or distracted. If we don't notice the results we were hoping to see fast enough, we get frustrated and then we give up.

Life has taught us that plans rarely go the way we think they will. For centuries, human beings have been making plans that just don't seem to work out. Psalm 94:11 says, "The LORD knows all human plans; he knows that they are futile." Even though they may be futile, we still try. If you are like most people, you planned for your career, your ministry, your family, your education, or your finances; and for a variety of reasons your plan just didn't happen the way you thought. As a result, we tend to develop an increasing reluctance toward planning, due to an expectation that "it will not work."

God does have a plan and His plan is to grow us. Philippians 1:6 reminds us that He is doing a work in each of us that He is eager to complete, but that plan requires our cooperation. Like the sailor on a sailboat, we must do our part to put up the sail and tie all the necessary knots in order to catch the winds that make it possible for our boat to sail. Dallas Willard wrote, "Grace is opposed to earning, but it is not opposed to effort."[1] Therefore, you can't do it alone, but neither will God. Connecting with God on our frequency (instead of randomly encountering Him) will require effort, and it will require a plan.

WHERE DO YOU START?

Assuming you want to know God and redirect your life to encounter Him regularly, how do you do it? For many people, it can sometimes seem like this:

Confusing—like a series of unconnected roads that intersect with no rhyme or reason. You have a desire to grow and connect with God on your frequency, but you don't know where to start. The task seems overwhelming. The issue is not bad intentions, shallowness, or lack of commitment. The issue is the lack of a good starting point.

Where you start is the key to the success of your plan. Most often, we start the formation of a plan by identifying the intended result and then working backward. This method can work when it comes to our finances, education, or our career. However, it rarely works in our attempt to connect with God on our frequency and experience spiritual growth.

Instead of starting at the end, start at the beginning. Start with the unique aspects of the way God created you. The best way to experience the results you are seeking is to know the One that created you in the way He created you, stay connected with Him regularly, and let Him produce the results. The unique components of who you are (your personality, spiritual pathway, learning style, etc.) are critical guideposts to accomplishing your mission. The planning process starts with your uniqueness. How did God create you to thrive? What types of activities raise the probability of your connecting with Him and what types of activities decrease it? How do you organize those things into a lifestyle that you can sustain?

Once you have identified some of the core components required to find your frequency, the next step is action—intelligent action. We have all heard the saying, "Insanity is doing the same thing over and over and expecting different results." Don't be insane. Don't continue trying the things you've always tried and expect different results. You'll tire out and drift further from your frequency. When you act, act intelligently with your uniqueness in mind.

Crafting a Plan

Put Some Structure to It

There are structured people and there are unstructured people. Hearing the word *structure* is enlivening for some and depressing for others. If you are not a structured person, don't stop reading! The type of structure we are proposing is more of a framework or reference point than it is a formulaic process. It is a value to live by, not a policy to adhere to. As William Paulsell, author and speaker on the topic of spiritual growth, writes, "It is unlikely that we will deepen our relationship with God in a casual or haphazard manner. There will be a need for some intentional commitment and some reorganization in our own lives. But, there is nothing that will enrich our lives more than a deeper, clearer perception of God's presence in the routine of daily life."[2]

The goal with every action, as it pertains to your spiritual growth, is progress—sustainable progress. The more successful an action is at connecting you with your frequency, the more likely you are going to want to repeat that action. That is what makes it sustainable in your life. Simple. Right? Unfortunately, many of us tend to associate spiritual actions with pain. We say, "Well, if it's boring, hard, and de-energizing, then it must be spiritual." Really? It doesn't have to be that way. Actually, if you are looking at it that way, you are completely missing the point.

God is the source of immeasurable energy, boundless inspiration, improbable heart change, and uncontainable joy.

It would be fair to expect that the things we do to connect with God should be invigorating. To be sure, not everything you try will be exciting. But some things will. And by understanding your personality, learning style, pathway to God, and primary sin that is blocking your frequency, you can narrow down the choices available to you, have a greater chance of finding success, and then repeat intelligent action.

FOUR AREAS OF ACTION

For the sake of clarity, we've identified four key areas of action to help you organize your approach to connecting with God on your frequency. These areas are not mind-blowingly innovative, but they are simple and functional as you take this next step.

Your Mind

Your mind is a significant channel that God uses to transform your heart. Romans 12:2 says, "Do not conform to the pattern of this world, but be transformed by the renewing of your mind. Then you will be able to test and approve what God's will is—his good, pleasing and perfect will." What types of things engage your mind? Books? Podcasts? Music? Art? Classes? Discussions? When you think back to a moment when you hit your frequency, what was capturing your mind? What type of environment were you in?

A. W. Tozer, author of *The Knowledge of the Holy*, writes,

"What comes into our minds when we think about God is the most important thing about us."[3] Therefore, it is important for you to select one thing or a combination of things that you know will captivate you, inspire the right kind of thoughts, increase your desire for God, and regularly contribute to living on your frequency. Approaching knowledge from the right perspective is very important. We should recognize that we will never fully understand everything about God. We should also be careful not to associate spiritual knowledge with spiritual growth, because knowledge does nothing to grow us if it does not translate to our heart, affecting the way we live. However, we can expect to learn things that will grow our heart and fuel our desire to courageously follow Jesus.

The Bible is foundational to this process. However, there are a lot of Christians who say, "I don't read my Bible enough" and then hang their heads. Maybe you have said that recently or you honestly think, *I don't read my Bible enough. I know I should, but I really don't want to and don't think I will.* Maybe you shouldn't simply *read* the Bible. Instead, maybe you should listen to it or teach it or memorize it or pray it or read it on your phone between meetings. Maybe you should try to absorb it when you are running, mowing, or doing the laundry. Maybe you need to target areas of Scripture that address what is blocking your frequency directly. Remember that God created you uniquely and you have a preferred learning style.

The types of actions that you pick will be important to your progress and the engagement of your mind.

It is essential that we fill our minds with thoughts of life, joy, peace, and purpose that can only come from God. Dallas Willard says, "The ultimate freedom we have as human beings is the power to select what we will allow or require our minds to dwell upon."[4] We have a freedom and a choice about our thoughts. Be intentional with that choice.

Your Time

Giving God the time, attention, and space to speak into your life is also critical. It is easy to live so fast-paced, preoccupied, and distracted that we crowd out the chance of hearing the voice of God. Everything we do takes time. We spend time doing all kinds of things like shopping, working, reading, and enjoying our hobbies. For the most part, what we spend our time doing is what captivates and drives our focus and attention. So when it comes to connecting with God on your frequency, you must realize that it takes time and you must spend time doing it.

Many of us feel like we don't have any more time left to spend. For a few of us, that's a true statement. Yet for most of us, what that really means is "I've already chosen to fill up my life with other things, and now I'm overbooked and overwhelmed." However, that problem doesn't have to be permanent. Time is like money, and we all spend money to get something in return. A wise man spends his money on things that provide a significant return. Time is a resource and we should look at it that way. God gives us a portion of time on earth that we can spend freely, and because time is limited, we need to be intentional with ways to spend our time that connect us with our frequency.

What types of things help you hear God's voice? As you think back to moments in your life when you hit your frequency, what were you doing? Your time is a tool to recalibrate and rediscover your frequency. Some people are able to spend hours each day reflecting on God. Other people only have minutes. Whatever the case, you must be intentional with your time as it relates to living on your frequency.

You can connect with God through prayer, reflection, journaling, silence in the car, or those nine minutes between when you hit the snooze button and when you actually have to get up. Be intentional. Ask God, "What do You want to tell me today?" Make it predictable, find what works, and strive toward sustainable action. Generally speaking, a short but regular time with God is better than an extended but random time with Him. Pick a practice and try it, keeping your spiritual pathway in mind. Did it help you hit your frequency? If not, try another one. Proverbs 8:17 says, "I love those who love me, and those who seek me find me." Seek Him with your time. It is a critical step.

Your Relationships

God often speaks most clearly through other people. Proverbs 27:17 says, "As iron sharpens iron, so one person sharpens another." Authentic community is a gift from God and an essential component of every person's life. What types of friendships do you have? What types of friendships do you want to have? What kinds of relational environments make you "light up" and feel energized?

Regardless of your preference, being in community is a nonnegotiable component of overall growth. No person was created to grow in isolation. From the beginning of time, God made it clear that we were not meant to live life alone. After God created Adam, He placed him in the garden of Eden and said, "It is not good for the man to be alone" (Gen. 2:18). Today, it is still not good for a person to be without relationship. Yet many of us move throughout our day, our week, or our lives alone.

We all long for a sense of connection through relationship. We want to be accepted, loved, and a part of something greater than ourselves—God planted these desires within us. However, it has been said that we can only be loved to the extent that we are known. If we are not fully known, then we cannot be fully loved. Yet being known feels risky. The thought, *If they knew everything about me, there is no way they would accept me*, keeps many of us from ever stepping into the sunlight of being discovered. So we remain partially known, partially accepted, and partially loved.

Our world is complicated and busy; therefore, connection with others is not easy. It will take grit and focus. We need others to confront, comfort, and commend us. We need a sounding board for ideas or a confidant in our struggle. Pick a way to connect with others that fits your personality and then be intentional. If you allow others to participate in your quest to live life on your frequency, you will be greatly blessed and be a blessing to others.

Your Experiences

Like you saw in Lindsay's story as she washed the homeless woman's feet, an experience can play a huge role in connecting with God on your frequency. Sometimes you meet God when you least expect it. Serving others is, and should be, core to a life lived on its frequency. You may have experienced this. When you serve others, you become less aware of the anxieties that consume you and become more aware of God's purpose.

Bob Buford, the founder of Leadership Network, insightfully said at an informal dinner gathering, "We find God's will for our lives in other people." When we serve others and live beyond ourselves, we begin to learn who we were created to be—and how to live on our frequency. One of the best things you can do to grow in your relationship with God is attend to the needs of others. How do you enjoy serving? What are you good at? What element of your personality would help others?

Too many Christians forget this component of their spiritual growth. James 2:26 says, "Faith without deeds is dead." You must give the fruit of your growth an opportunity to flourish and edify others. Experiencing the joy in serving others is absolutely necessary for each of us to experience the life that Jesus promised. Pick a place to serve that fits your pathway to God and personality strengths. Be consistent. You will be surprised how serving experiences that are aligned with the way you are designed help you hit your frequency.

Shared Elements of Frequency

When we first began to think about how frequency works in peoples' lives, we discovered some research about happiness and fulfillment that was surprising but rang true. According to the research, the words people use to describe happiness and fulfillment are similar in a wide spectrum of contexts even though the activities that contributed to the sense of fulfillment were very different.[5] A long-distance swimmer describes the joy she feels when swimming the same way others describe playing an instrument skillfully, caring for a newborn, solving a math problem, or fixing a car. We are all different, and the various combinations of learning styles, pathways, and personalities accentuate each person's unique frequency to God. However, there are some shared elements that are true about every person when finding his or her frequency.

Crafting a Plan

A Challenge Only You Can Do

Most people hit their frequency when they are engaged in something that challenges their unique set of skills to accomplish a given task. Think about it. You see this throughout Scripture: David and his slingshot, Sampson and his strength, Noah and his construction, and Paul and his communication skills. When you are tuning into your frequency, it will likely involve a type of challenge that you are uniquely qualified or wired to accomplish. That is why you may experience God in an activity that would completely frustrate someone else.

A Goal to Achieve

A random encounter with God can be expected to happen every now and then. When you have a specific goal in mind, you have a higher chance of hitting your frequency predictably. We, as Christians, have gotten used to the mind-set of doing a list of activities because we are supposed to do them. Most of those activities are wonderful and helpful things, but they lack a clear end point—an intended goal. Without a goal, these once-helpful activities become routine and meaningless. For example, being in nature might be a great way for you to connect with God, but if you are playing a frustrating round of golf or cursing the weeds as you pull them from your landscaping, you are likely not going to experience God in those moments. Reading your Bible or a good book is a great idea, but doing it just to do it, rather than as a means to encounter God, probably won't work. Intentional, specific, and measurable goals are usually a consistent element of people who regularly live on their frequency.

Concrete Action That Is Attainable

The goals you set must be possible. If you set out to run a marathon with no training, you'll fail spectacularly. When it comes to following Jesus, we can set out to be a saint and fall flat on our face. Life is a journey of incremental steps toward noticeable improvement. Anyone who has lived on this earth long enough will tell you that every time they think they've "arrived," God shows or reveals something brand new about His greatness and/or the area they need to grow. If you set out to be a spiritual hero and expect results overnight, you will be confused by what reality brings. Set a goal that is realistic and sustainable; otherwise, you are destined to fail.

Attitude of Surrender

Consistently living on your frequency is marked by a life of humility. James 4:6 says, "God opposes the proud but shows favor to the humble." A willingness to try anything, to discover new truths, and to live with a spirit of grace toward yourself and others should be the norm. Nothing can happen without surrender. Jesus said that if you want to find your life, you must lose it (Matt. 10:39). You have to give up control, surrender everything to the loving leadership of the God who knows best. David Benner, author of *Surrender to Love*, says, "Far from being a sign of weakness, only surrender brings us to Someone bigger, better, and stronger than we are—the only One who is strong enough to free us from the prison of egocentricity."[6]

An attitude of surrender and humility inevitably comes when we grasp the vastness of God, the brokenness of our situation, and the price that was paid by Jesus to redeem that situation. Remember that you are God's creation. You are His masterpiece. He wants to see you living on your frequency, surrendered to Him, and experiencing life at its fullest.

AIM SMALL, MISS SMALL

During the Revolutionary War, rifles were not very accurate. Soldiers would load them, point them in a direction, and hope to hit something in the vicinity of where they were aiming. This made battles gruesome because opposing armies needed to stand so close to their opponent in order to inflict the intended damage.

Because rifles at that time were so inaccurate, principles of aim began to emerge. One of those principles is helpful to the way we approach connecting with God on our frequency. When soldiers were taught how to aim, they were instructed to "aim small." If you aim small, you miss small. For example, if a soldier aims at a target and misses, then he would have completely missed the target. However, if he aimed at a specific dot on the target and missed the dot, then he would still hit the target.

When it comes to our spiritual growth (or any plan for that matter), we have a tendency to aim too big. We aim for a dream of what could/should be instead of deliberately trusting God to improve our daily reality. There is nothing wrong with dreaming big—but just like a Revolutionary War soldier, if you aim big and miss, you may also miss your goal. Conversely, if you aim for the proverbial dot on the target and miss, you will still make significant progress toward the goal. When you aim small, you miss small.

Specific, targeted, concrete action toward connecting with God is your best chance for success. When you miss, you will only miss slightly. Ultimately, this will help you hone in on the best type of action for the best type of results in your spiritual journey, narrowing the gap of time you spend living off your frequency.

MAKING AN ETERNAL DIFFERENCE

This is all for a point. God wants to use your life. There is a watching world that is paying attention to the lives of those that claim to follow Jesus. Are we any different? Do we have the joy that we talk about and are we changing the way we say we are? Do our lives benefit the lives of others and our communities? Will we make an eternal difference?

Real personal, social, and cultural change starts with the grace of Jesus. Through Him, we are able to change the world. Jesus said, "Those who remain in me, and I in them, will produce much fruit. For apart from me you can do nothing" (John 15:5 NLT).

If we forget that we are broken people who have recurring sin and need grace and forgiveness, we can lose our motivation or begin doing things with the wrong motivation (impressing others, making ourselves feel good, etc.). If we don't have an intimate relationship with the One who created and saved us, then we are merely activists. There is, of course, nothing wrong with being an activist, but as Christ-followers, our energy will eventually dry up because we will be living on our own power and off our frequency with God.

It is important for each of us to continue to grow in our love for God and the causes that result from that love. We will be passionate about helping others because of our gratitude for the way God helped (and is helping) us. Imagine every person living on his or her frequency—encountering the living God on a daily basis. Imagine the fruit. Imagine the absence of pain and sin. Imagine the joy and authentic community. Imagine the gospel—alive and well in every corner of this world. Imagine the justice. Imagine the love. This, my friends, would be heaven on earth.

SOME THOUGHTS BEFORE MOVING ON

You have a frequency that is different than everyone else. But here is the most important lesson of all: your frequency is not about you.

On the surface, this statement seems to fly in the face of the whole idea we are talking about. After all, it is *your* frequency, *your* difference, and *your* uniqueness. Sure, finding your frequency starts with discovering elements about you, but living on your frequency cannot end with you. In *The Purpose Driven Life*, Rick Warren captures this challenge: "The purpose of your life is far greater than your own personal fulfillment, your peace of mind, or even your happiness. It's far greater than your family, your career, or even your wildest dreams and ambitions. If you want to know why you were placed on this planet, you must begin with God. You were born *by* His purpose and *for* His purpose."[7]

Your frequency has a big *so that* attached to it. The *so that* is not about looking good, feeling good, or achieving more than someone else. God designed your unique frequency so that you can participate in His redemptive work in ways you otherwise could not. So that you can live a life full of the transformative grace and power of Jesus, experiencing it yourself and sharing it with everyone around you. So that you may have life and have it more abundantly. Find your frequency and live on it so that a watching world will see God at work in your life and be compelled to pursue their frequency too.

So let's get started! It is time to discover your learning style, pathway to God, personality, and primary sin that blocks your frequency. You have what it takes to grow. God has given you everything you need. Living on your frequency begins now.

Chapter 5

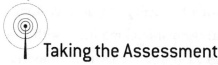

Taking the Assessment

You can live on your frequency, and we are excited for you to take the next step. We have both spent years working on a project called Monvee—our best attempt at helping people find their frequency and then live on it. Now that you have learned about your frequency and what it takes to find it, we want you to experience Monvee. We know it will help.

WHAT IS MONVEE?

Monvee (www.monvee.com) combines solid theology with innovative technology to deliver a tool that helps people with resources, ways to spend their time, powerful experiences, and relational connections that fit the unique way God designed them to grow. Monvee started in 2007 with a passion to help people connect their desire to grow in their relationship with God with a plan. It started in a local church with the intent to help people answer the question, "How do I go deeper?"

Going deeper doesn't necessarily mean reading thicker books. It means living life on your frequency, where every day is filled with memorable, transformational moments with God.

Monvee is designed to help you understand important components of your frequency and help you craft a plan to live on it. With this book, we have included access to a free Monvee assessment called the Monvee Discovery, which is based on 780 questions boiled down to 22 easy-to-answer questions that will help apply the concepts you have read about in this book. Through years of research and thousands of experiments, we know that the Monvee Discovery is precise in helping people.

Let's Get Started!

The Monvee Discovery process is innovative, accurate, and fun. When you get your results after the assessment, you will see your learning style, pathway to God, personality type, and the primary spiritual inhibitor that blocks your frequency.

Get Your Code

You have a free assessment code that was included with the purchase of this book (see the sealed insert in the opening pages). This code is for one-time use, because it is specific to you. Once you have located your code, go to monvee.com, click on "Login," and get started.

Complete the Assessment

While the Monvee Discovery Process is designed to only take about ten minutes, don't feel rushed. Take your time, have fun, and be honest. The more honest you are, the more accurate it will be. Your information is confidential and protected. If you get stuck or aren't sure what to do next, click the green help box located in the top left corner on your screen.

Your Discovery Summary

Once you have completed the Monvee Discovery Process, you will receive an e-mail with a personalized Discovery Summary. Take time to review the summary and read through the unique aspects of the way God made you. Share your Discovery Summary with others to spark conversation, receive feedback, and hear additional input about what you learned.

Find Your Chapter

The nine remaining chapters of *Frequency* are organized around the nine major personality categories that Monvee measures. Each of the personality styles is associated with a different person from the Bible. After finding out through your Discovery Summary what biblical personality you are most similar to, flip to the corresponding chapter. This is *your* chapter—filled with insight and perspectives that specifically apply to you. Also, each chapter has an interview with an author, leader, or pastor who happens to share the same personality style as you. After you read your chapter, read through the interviews of all the other chapters as well. Each interviewee will discuss personal stories, thoughts, and recommendations for growth as they pertain to the unique ways that God has made them. You will certainly find nuggets of wisdom and truth for yourself.

DISCOVER OTHERS' PERSONALITY STYLES

Once you have finished your chapter, find out about the elements of frequency for those around you. Encourage people who are closest to you to take the free Monvee assessment that can be accessed through their own *Frequency* book. Then find their chapter and learn about how God made them. We think that these chapters will provide powerful insight and spark conversation in ways that will surprise you. Use these chapters to better understand your spouse or significant other, your kids, your inner circle of friends, your small group, or your coworkers. Try writing the personality type for some of those people in the space below.

Keep Track

My spouse (or significant other)

My son/daughter

My friend

My friend

Other

Other

Other

If you are a pastor and would like to learn how you can help the people in your church discover their frequency and then live on it in a way that is connected to the church, go to www.monvee.com/pastors.

SOME THOUGHTS BEFORE MOVING ON

Discovery is key to living on your frequency. Through the Monvee Discovery Process, you will learn more about yourself, which, in turn, will help you experience sustainable success in your spiritual growth and pursue God with full abandon. God has designed you to live on your frequency—connected to Him. Now it's time to get started!

PART 2

YOUR PERSONALITY STYLE

Chapter 6

Joseph

Pete Wilson and Jenni Catron

Joseph was a confident, outspoken dreamer and a man of principle. He overcame many difficulties in his life, including being betrayed by his brothers, sold into captivity, and being unjustly accused, demoted, and imprisoned. However, God was with Joseph and honored his commitment to integrity and godliness. Joseph was entrusted with great authority and responsibility at a time when many people needed his help. He was able to provide that help for others through the fruit of his careful planning and deep wisdom. Eventually, he was reconciled with the brothers who betrayed him and trusted that God had been working His good plan all along. Joseph is a great example of a man who had steadfast conviction but allowed God to channel his temper and bless his patience.

ELEMENTS OF YOUR PERSONALITY

If you have a Joseph personality, you are able to overcome adversity and you have a very strong moral compass. You are a person of confidence who is comfortable talking about what you believe, even if others disagree. Giving yourself to a higher cause motivates you as you seek truth, integrity, and justice.

You may find yourself feeling overly fearful of being seen as corrupt or dishonest, so you work hard to be a person of character and integrity. You are able to resist temptation and do what is right. You are organized at home and work because you love your life a particular way. Some might call you a perfectionist; you prefer to be called prepared. You are motivated to improve and fix the world around you. You love to be right and you work hard to justify your work and ideas. You love to tackle a challenge and to overcome. You pursue high standards and values, even if it requires sacrifice.

You are disciplined and believe that living a strict life is the best way to live. While this leads to a life that is guided by principle, it can make trusting your feelings or going with your gut difficult for you.

The Best of You

You are disciplined, strong, responsible, wise, organized, and discerning. You love the idea of truth and have built your life around trying to live by God's truth. You take His Word very seriously and make concerted efforts to live by it. People see you as a person of deep and honest integrity. Some may call you idealistic or even high-minded because you love a good cause to believe in.

The Other Side of You

Principle and discipline can turn into perfectionism and result in a judgmental spirit. You will always walk a fine line of telling the truth to those around you and judging. Also, be aware of your workload, because your work ethic can lead you to become a workaholic. You can get so caught up in what you're doing that you can appear impersonal, unsympathetic, and cold.

The Primary Spiritual Inhibitor That Blocks Your Frequency: Anger

You have a tendency to experience strong feelings of annoyance, displeasure, or hostility toward people or circumstances. You can become easily frustrated with other people's actions, especially if you disagree with them. Anger is often expressed verbally or physically, but in some cases it is stuffed inside and eventually grows into bitterness or resentment. Surges of anger can quickly distract your spiritual growth and attentiveness to God's voice.

MEET SOME PEOPLE LIKE YOU

Pete Wilson. Pete is the founding and lead pastor of Cross Point Church in Nashville, Tennessee. Pete is the author of *Plan B,*[1] blogs regularly at withoutwax.tv, and is a sought-after speaker.

Jenni Catron. Jenni is the executive director at Cross Point Church in Nashville, Tennessee. She blogs regularly at jennicatron.tv and is the founder of Cultivate Her.

Tell us a little bit about CrossPoint.

PETE. Cross Point is a nine-year-old church located in the Nashville area. We started as a portable church in a school cafeteria. As we grew and quickly became out of space, we embraced the multisite model. We have five campuses now. Our goal is to create a biblical community of people who are growing together and trying to reach people around the world with the gospel.

How have you seen your personality affect your spiritual growth?

PETE. I love how Joseph lived his life. He faced many different challenges that he had to overcome. He always seemed to be backed up against the wall, yet he was always able to overcome. When Joseph was in the bottom of the pit or falsely accused of rape or in prison feeling forgotten, he continued to have faith and chose to trust in God. In those moments in my life, I feel closest to God. Like Joseph, I feel like I always have this consistent feeling that "God is able." Even when it doesn't seem to make sense from the outside, I have an idealistic faith. It is not hard for me to believe that God is in control and He is working His plan.

JENNI. I always turn everything into a goal. It is how I am wired. I have always been a planner, even as a kid. I had everything planned, organized, and structured. As an adult now who is married and helping lead a large church, the desire to do everything right oftentimes overwhelms and frustrates me. I think, *I'm not doing everything I could do* or *I'm not doing everything as well as I ought to.*

In my spiritual life, I fight the tension between making it a list of tasks to check and a real, authentic relationship with God. The more complex life has gotten, the more I feel like I don't have time for any quiet moments with God. I feel like I have too much to do. I like having responsibility and being productive; however, I've had to learn to channel that into my spiritual life. I love to run. Running has been a great way for me to be both productive and reflective. As I run, I can soak in the nature around me or listen to a worship album on my iPod. There are definitely times that I need to just slow down and stop accomplishing stuff. But there are other times when I can be productive while spending focused time with God.

How have you seen anger block your frequency?

PETE. I think understanding your "frequency blocker" is really important because we all have the capacity for self-deception. Proverbs 14:12 says, "There is a way that appears to be right, but in the end it leads to death." It's so easy to get comfortable with our sin. We all see the dark side of sin the world, while ignoring the struggle with our own sin. It's important for people to be aware of sin because it is an incredible reminder of how much we need a Savior. Obviously, I am not proud of my signature sin, but it reminds me every time about how much I need Jesus pulsating through my veins—if I want to live the life He has called me to live.

JENNI. I have a terrible tendency to stuff my frustrations instead of working through them. My husband will sometimes say, "Jen, why didn't you tell me? Why did you hold on to that for so long?" I don't even realize I am holding on to something. Sometimes, I think there is a prideful arrogance that believes I can handle it without any help; I can solve it by myself. Anger affects my life in a variety of ways, for sure. And most times, I struggle to realize it.

How do you confront anger?

PETE. For me, it comes down to complete honesty. I have to be willing to be publicly honest. A few years ago, our church was going through a lot of transition. We were experiencing fantastic growth and we transitioned to a multisite strategy with several multisite pastors. So my role was changing dramatically. We had chosen to empower our campus pastors to do the things that I had always enjoyed and loved doing. In order for it to work well, I needed to step back so that our campus pastors could step up to be effective at the campus they were leading.

I remember one specific moment when I felt my "frequency blocker" surface. We were doing a baptism service, and like most pastors, I love being a part of baptism services. Because we had transitioned most of the hands-on leadership responsibilities to the campus pastors, we had them do all the baptisms. I was there and present, but I wasn't in the water. Our Nashville campus pastor, Blake, was in the water, experiencing the joy of the moment. They were hugging and high-fiving each person who was baptized, but I was standing on the side holding cue cards with names on them for the people in the pool. As I was holding up the cards, I felt sin come over my heart.

I remember thinking, *I shouldn't be doing this. I deserve better than this. That should be me in there baptizing those people.* And for me, the only way I could battle that type of sin was to admit it at the campus pastor meeting the next day. I honestly told them what was going through my mind during the baptisms. When I should have been celebrating the incredible moment for all these people, I was thinking about myself and letting my anger take over.

When I took it out of the darkness and brought it into the light, I felt like the power of that sin was gone. It comes back, of course, in different situations, but I was able to sort through what I was feeling that day. Sin grows momentum in the dark. However, if I drag it out and become transparent with it, it instantaneously dies.

JENNI. A counselor once told me to journal my feelings. Journal my feelings? I don't think so. I said, "I'm not journaling my feelings. Journals are for documentation and planning, not feelings." Regardless of what I thought about it, she made me do it. And it worked. As I wrote down my frustrations, anger, and sources of bitterness, I was able to acknowledge them for what they are. The journal became a place for me to see what was eating at my heart and stop letting it fester there. It sounds cheesy, but it has worked for me.

What are some personal-growth recommendations for people like you?

PETE. First, find what works.

I used to struggle with prayer. I'm so easily distracted. My prayer times were great for the first sixty seconds and then after that, it was all downhill. I started thinking of a million different things and creating a to-do list. I would try getting back to my prayer only to have the same thing happen again. So I gave up.

Then a few years ago on a mission trip, I discovered prayer walks. On the trip, the goal was to walk around a city block and pray for the people. I had never heard of a prayer walk. But all of a sudden, I discovered that I could pray when I was walking, moving, and was outside. It allowed me to see and experience my surroundings, which fueled my prayers. Now when I feel like I need to spend an extended period of time in prayer, I take a walk. If I'm in a place with beautiful surroundings, I can pray for two or three hours at a time. Remember to be flexible with what types of activities you choose and then experiment until you find something that works.

JENNI. My recommendation is, just say it.

Start being open with people you trust, even if you don't have the perfect words. Sometimes my husband will catch me with my wheels turning—lost in thought. Because of my perfectionistic nature, I try to work through all the details in my head before I say anything out loud. I want to say it perfectly. There is definitely wisdom in choosing your words carefully and not just saying whatever. But I go to the other extreme to make sure it is polished, so that I look polished. Sharing your weaknesses and struggles is not always going to be pretty or perfect. Be vulnerable, and just say it. The people closest to you will understand if you don't say it exactly the way you mean it. Give yourself some grace, and they will too.

PETE. Also, take a Sabbath.

One of the things about people who are wired like me is that they are constantly motivated to try to improve and fix things. We are hardwired to want to overcome challenges. As a result, we can become addicted to productivity. Productivity can be a dangerous drug where you get addicted to the feeling of being productive. For me, the Sabbath (or taking a day off from anything productive) has become an incredible discipline to my spiritual growth.

Do you have any final thoughts?

PETE. When it comes to your spiritual life, you have to realize that there is no such thing as a cookie-cutter soul. We have all been wired differently. It is part of the beauty of God's creativity that we connect with God in different ways. Unfortunately, too many approaches to spiritual growth have a cookie-cutter approach. It just doesn't work. I think a lot of people feel guilty about their lack of spiritual growth because what they have been told to do doesn't match the way they are wired. Taking the time to figure out how you are wired and finding a unique plan for yourself is so important. It may take some deep study to discover that.

I don't have all the answers, but I do know that souls don't develop in cookie-cutter fashion. Churches were never intended to be factories where we crank out people who are always in the same place at the same time. We have to take responsibility as a church and as individuals to find that unique plan for us and work that unique plan. Because you are a Joseph, you will be tempted to just fill your life with activities. Be careful to select the right kind of activities so that you experience the growth you desire.

JENNI. Let go of what you think other people want from you. Try to get a glimpse of what God really thinks about you and then pursue that. You have to let go of those preconceived paths, ideas, and routes to hear God's voice. God speaks to each of us uniquely and specifically according to our unique design. Galatians 6:4 says, "Make a careful exploration of who you are and the work you have been given" (MSG). Take the time to understand who you are, how you were created, and how God equipped you with the experiences and opportunities in your life. He has good plans for you. Trust Him completely.

PETE AND JENNI'S RESOURCE RECOMMENDATIONS

Nouwen, Henri. *The Way of the Heart.* New York: Harper-One, 1991.

Barton, Ruth Haley. *Strengthening the Soul of Your Leadership.* Downers Grove, IL: InterVarsity Press, 2008.

Ortberg, John. *The Me I Want to Be.* Grand Rapids: Zondervan, 2009.

Allender, Dan. *Sabbath.* Nashville: Thomas Nelson, 2009.

Maxwell, John. *The 21 Most Powerful Minutes in a Leader's Day.* Nashville: Thomas Nelson, 2009.

SOME THOUGHTS BEFORE MOVING ON

If you are like Joseph, here are some suggestions for you:

- Be sure to spend some time at least once a week doing something you love. Play a sport, drink your favorite coffee, watch a movie, meet a friend, or go for a walk.

- Pick a drawer or closet and allow it to be messy.

- Replace the phrase "I should" with "I want to" or "I don't want to."

- Remember that it is okay for you to relax and enjoy yourself. It is also okay for you to make mistakes.

- Recognize that anger is a normal emotion. Ask God and those around you if there is something beneath your anger that you are not aware of. Some great ways to express anger are writing, talking it out with a close friend, or exercising.

Chapter 7

Abraham

Matt Werner

Abraham was generous, faith-filled, and others-centered. He would give the tunic off his back to anyone who needed his help. His nephew Lot, more than anyone, owed much of the blessing in his life to Abraham's helpful, giving spirit. When their herds had multiplied beyond what their land could support, Abraham gave Lot the first choice of the new piece of land. Abraham was willing to do anything in obedience to God, even sacrifice his only son, which is why Abraham is considered the "father of faith." God promised Abraham a steadfast legacy, a multitude of descendants, and a covenant unlike any other. Abraham was blessed because of his faith, his commitment to God's plan for his life, and his willingness to do anything for others.

Elements of Your Personality

If you have an Abraham personality, your caring nature is your hallmark. You are a good listener and in tune with how those around you feel. You relate well with others, and you make friends easily. People who are close to you see you as generous, playful, and sincere. You make people feel important and loved. Some of what people love about you is that you have an uncanny ability to see the best in them and to meet their needs in specific, helpful ways. You help them believe that there is more to them than what they can see. You pride yourself on being transparent and want to be known as much as you want to know others. Being fearful of feeling unwanted and/or unloved, you are motivated to find ways to show love and you want to feel needed and wanted.

The Best of You

You are altruistic, generous, enthusiastic, and thoughtful. You think of others first and are unselfish. Those who know you see you as nurturing, encouraging, and filled with genuine interest in them. You love to give a hug, pat someone on the back, or say an encouraging word. You find pleasure in pitching in and helping people when they ask. You would never think of standing by and watching while someone else was in need of a helping hand.

The Other Side of You

Because you have such a strong need to help others, you find it hard to say no and can become exhausted. Sometimes you believe that the only way to receive love and affection is to earn it. You can spend too much time trying to impress people and find yourself working to please everyone too much. Be careful to remember that God loves you not for what you do for Him, but because you are who He made you to be.

The Primary Spiritual Inhibitor That Blocks Your Frequency: Pride

You have the tendency to allow your generosity or kind actions to become selfishly motivated. If you give only to get something back, you may become resentful and punishing toward others if your expectations are unfulfilled. Being known as a "helpful" person is very important to you. Because you can meet needs so effectively, there is a danger of becoming self-important and developing a feeling of being owed. Guard against overrating yourself and concentrate on your genuine desire to help people.

MEET SOMEONE LIKE YOU

Matt Werner. Matt Werner is the spiritual formation director at Salem Lutheran Church outside of Houston, Texas. Matt has successfully implemented Monvee at Salem Lutheran and has a passion for growth of individuals in their congregation.

What are you working on these days?

MATT. I'm at Salem Lutheran Church in Tomball, Texas. We are a very young, family-orientated church. I have been there for four years. I started off as a worship leader and I really enjoyed that. Then I began to have the desire to be in more of a pastoral role at the church. So I recently became the spiritual formation director and I love it.

When you read your Monvee Discovery Summary for the first time, were there particular things that felt affirming?

MATT. The most affirming thing for me was reading about my spiritual inhibitor. I remember thinking, *Yeah, that is totally correct.* I literally laughed out loud as I was reading it to one of my friends because it perfectly described how I typically sin. That has been my experience with a lot of people when they take the Monvee assessment. I will sit down with someone and say, "Hey, take this." They sit down, take the assessment, get the results, and just laugh. I don't think they expect it to be so accurate. When I got the result, "You have the tendency to be prideful and use generosity to manipulate others." I was shocked. It hit me like a ton of bricks. Honestly, it really validated the Monvee tool for me and made me want our whole church to experience it.

I struggle in some other areas as well, but I'm realizing

that, for me, it is all rooted in my pride. I don't think I would have been able to say or identify that before. Now it makes perfect sense.

Is it a struggle for you and people like you to talk about their spiritual inhibitor?

MATT. I doubt that it's natural for anybody, especially in the context of ministry. But, yes, I do think it is hard. I mean, come on, we struggle with pride (and what others think of us) the most. The last thing I'd want to do is shatter my image. Even though it is awkward, I have chosen to be bold about my struggle with pride to our congregation. Being in front of a crowd, for me, is absolutely a breeding ground for my pride. So it has been cool to make myself a real person to my congregation in a safe way. Having that self-awareness and admitting to my peers has had a positive effect on my ministry and teaching, for sure.

Was there anything in your Monvee Discovery Summary that surprised you?

MATT. I have been a worship leader for years. So I naturally thought my pathway to God would be corporate worship. When I saw that it was creation, I thought, "Well, that's interesting." As I have had more time to think about it, I've realized that it is absolutely true. I do love, love, love the outdoors.

I remember fishing with my father and brothers when I was a kid. I would just look around and be enamored with the creation around us. God's creation reminds me of how small I am, helping me identify my self-centeredness. So, for me, creation is a wonderful pathway, especially when it is paired with my inhibitor.

What are some recommendations for personal growth for people like you?

MATT. First, serve someone who can't give back.

Intentionally serving someone who has nothing to offer me back is a key way to keep my pride in check. I have the tendency to only seek out opportunities to serve others or "give back" when my actions make me look good or noble to others. My pastor pointed out this flaw to me one time. Early on in ministry, I built volunteer teams of seemingly successful, highly influential people, and I intentionally avoided people who weren't. In a weird way, it made me feel better about myself and made me look like a better leader. But finally my pastor said, "Who do you have on your team that is not highly influential or successful?"

Obviously, surrounding yourself with talented people is not a bad thing. But his question forced me to see what was happening within myself. I had become accustomed to surrounding myself with people who could help me out in some way. As an Abraham, it is important to intentionally serve people who have nothing to offer me. Abraham did this when he prayed for Sodom, a city that had nothing to offer him. I want to do the same by truly looking out for other people's interests in ways that don't directly benefit me.

Second, let someone else get the credit.

Although it is completely against my nature, I need to regularly let someone else have the advantage or get the credit. There are moments when I feel like I deserve it, but deciding to consciously dismiss that thought has been critical for my ability to grow. Even though Abraham was blessed and "deserved" to have his choice in God's blessing, he gave Lot the choice of the land that had been given to them. He let Lot have the advantage.

For me, I have to consciously choose to support others in what they are doing, making them look good. If I am only being generous or serving others because it makes me feel good about myself or because I will be seen as a servant, then I need to check my motives. People who are like Abraham naturally have a servant's heart and habitually try to help others succeed. However, we may not always get credit for our actions. Let that be okay. God sees what you are doing and that should be enough.

Finally, discover your true worth.

Abraham and Sarah waited almost a decade for the birth of their first son. God had promised Abraham to bless him through his descendants, so Isaac, their son, was a long-anticipated blessing. Isaac resembled, in a way, Abraham's worth—his legacy. But, Abraham was willing to lay down that worth when God asked him to provide Isaac as a sacrifice. Abraham obeyed, but he was eventually stopped by an angel.

In a sense, Abraham said, "God, You establish my worth. Not what I do, what I have done, or what I have created. Do with me what You want, even if it appears that I have nothing left besides You." God honored his humble, surrendered heart and his steadfast acknowledgment of where he received his true worth. I must remember that God gives me my worth, not the affections of people, and you should too. It is a very, very difficult lesson to learn.

Do you have any final thoughts for people like you?

MATT. You absolutely have to get to the place in your heart where you realize that God has a better plan for you than you have for yourself. I have heard that phrase my whole life, and most people who have grown up in church have. But it is huge to truly believe that God wants to give you the desires of your heart. Your desires for yourself will never, ever, ever come close to what He has intended for you.

Look at Abraham. He had it all before God called him. He was already rich, he was already blessed, and he had his whole life going for him. However, he went from the self-made life to the God-made life, where he finally got to sit under God's blessings instead of his own blessings. Here's the funny thing: both lives were lives of prosperity and success. And they both went from blessing to blessing. But the difference is, one was a perceived obedience and the other was a real obedience. They looked similar at first, but they were not the same in the long run. There will always be choices centered on me (immediate) versus choices centered on God (long-term). It is definitely a wrestle, but once you get a grip on what you struggle with, God will totally use you and deal with your pride.

God will break you for your own good. When you break because of your own pride, it can be ugly. But when you break because of God's work in you, it is beautiful and inherently healing to your core. God may say, "I absolutely have to take you to the desert in order to accomplish what I want to accomplish in you," but it will be worth it in the end.

Spend less time grabbing for the plan and the life you want. And remember the prayer, "Who am I that You are mindful of me?" That is the right place to get to—the place where you can actually say, "Okay, God, this is about You." You don't want to have to wait until you ruin or break your life on your own. Let Him break you now; you want the good kind of breaking.

MATT'S RESOURCE RECOMMENDATIONS

Stanley, Andy. *The Enemies of the Heart.* Sisters, OR: Multnomah Books, 2011.

Patrick, Darrin. *Church Planter.* Wheaton, IL: Crossway Books, 2010.

The Village Church Weekly Podcast by Matt Chandler

Breakaway Ministries Weekly Podcast by Ben Stuart

Redeemer Presbyterian Weekly Podcast by Tim Keller

SOME THOUGHTS BEFORE MOVING ON

If you are like Abraham, here are some suggestions for you:

- You are thought of as a people person. While it is true that you receive energy from being with others, try engaging in some activities that you love to do alone. Use the time alone to focus on what God might be speaking to you and what your needs might be.

- Next time someone compliments you or directs praise your way, say thank you instead of deflecting the praise or explaining why it wasn't really you.

- It is important to remember that God loves you— period. You don't have to do anything for that. You do not have to give to be loved; you are loved.

- Intentionally ask someone for help, instead of always being the one helping.

- Frequency is so important for you to embrace. Instead of trying to please everyone around you, focus on connecting with God on your frequency.

Chapter 8

Jacob

Tony Wood and Brad Lomenick

Jacob was a talented and charismatic hard worker. He was a great patriarch whose eventual descendant was Jesus. Jacob spent his life striving to achieve great things any way he could. Throughout his life, Jacob charmed, labored, and strategized his way to success. He found a shrewd way to inherit his brother's birthright by trading him a bowl of stew, he worked in the fields for fourteen years to earn his wife's hand in marriage, and he won a wrestling match with an angel. He was loved by God and chosen for a great destiny. That destiny came true when he presented himself in an honest way before God, while following instructions obediently.

ELEMENTS OF YOUR PERSONALITY

If you have a Jacob personality, typically speaking, you are internally driven to succeed. Your definition of success likely comes from what you were taught to value, but in the end, you will strive to be "somebody," in whatever way you define that. You tend to be ambitious, industrious, confident, and energetic. People see you as self-confident, as well as gracious.

You have a strong desire to feel valuable, to do meaningful things, and to be recognized for it. Therefore, you are able to overcome obstacles easily. You are motivated by affirmation from those around you, by the attention of others, and by the admiration of your peers. You work hard to impress people you know and people you don't know. You succeed often, and people like to be around you because you believe in yourself. You work hard to develop the natural talents and abilities God gave you. Others are drawn to your zest for life, your problem-solving ability, and your willingness to be out front.

The Best of You

You are made to accomplish and perform well. God can use your wiring to accomplish great work for His kingdom. You are a natural leader both functionally and morally because people like to follow and work with you to accomplish great things. You are winsome with others, which helps you accomplish your goals. Your optimism and faith are contagious, and you love the idea of a comeback. Rebounding from setbacks and resiliency are part of the fabric of your character.

The Other Side of You

Pleasing people can be exhausting and, at times, confusing to your sense of who you are. It can be easy to manicure your image of strength, even though you may feel weak. You have a tendency toward self-centeredness and caring for others in a way that brings you reward. You are right most of the time; however, you can have a hard time admitting when you are wrong. You can be resistant to constructive criticism if you don't trust the messenger. When you feel threatened, you will resort to superficial interactions and shallow conversations.

The Primary Spiritual Inhibitor That Blocks Your Frequency: Deception

You have a tendency to manage your image by overstating the truth, covering your faults, or avoiding situations that reveal your weaknesses. You may or may not outright lie, but you are tempted to distort the truth to make yourself look better. "Getting ahead" or leveraging your leadership ability for personal gain are potential pitfalls.

MEET SOME PEOPLE LIKE YOU

Tony Wood. Tony is the founding and teaching pastor of Moment Church in Orange County, California. Before starting Moment Church, Tony led a thriving student ministry in Corona, California, called Generate.

Brad Lomenick. Brad is the president, executive director, and vision caster of Catalyst. Catalyst hosts leadership events primarily for young leaders. He lives in Atlanta, Georgia.

What would you say to people who are like Jacob?

TONY. Monvee's description of the Jacob personality talks about the future-oriented, innovative, visionary, objective, and resilient leader. It's great to have that personality. Many great leaders have had a desire to do something bold and audacious, but I think it is important to address and pay attention to your motive. Your Monvee profile points out you can be industrious, confident, energetic, but you can do it for all the wrong reasons if you are not careful. It comes down to your motive and your heart.

I have found the only way to battle my motives as they relate to my ambition is to be working from a foundational base of humility. I have to remind myself that this is God's show and I am just a small part of it. I need to submit to His great design and His great will, always being kingdom-oriented first. So even when the good and natural parts of your personality take over, make sure your motives are founded in humility.

What can be a challenge about being a Jacob?

BRAD. I tend to make everything a competition, even spiritual disciplines. If I am reading through Ephesians, Philippians, or Colossians, I try to become an expert in that field in comparison with people around me. So I approach most activities with the mind-set, "How can I conquer this?" Growth, for somebody like me, is way more action-oriented and solution-minded. I like to check things off so that I feel like I executed well. My inability to sit still and soak in God's truth can be a challenge for me.

I have to be intentional to allow Scripture to soak in when I read it. It's not a competition. When I spend time alone, I've been trying to think about the verses I'm reading not for how I'm going to use them, but for how God is going to use them in me. It's important for me to stop and let God speak.

Tony. One of the challenges I face is a lack of patience. It comes with my drive to achieve. If I'm not careful, I can drive my own soul into insanity. It can definitely destroy families. However, there is hope in a Jacob personality. When Jacobs are truly relinquished to God's plan—wow, amazing things can happen. The boldness of a Jacob gives me hope. We are not afraid to confront the gates of hell, we are not afraid to take risks, and we are not afraid to lose all things and count the costs. A Jacob can be an oak tree that is vibrant because he or she is willing to stand against the elements—the rain, the wind, and the storm.

That being said, there are times where I have gone home and said, "I want to quit." That is hard for me to admit. I just thought I wanted to quit, work for Starbucks, release the pressure that I feel, and make double-pump vanilla lattes. I think I can nail that job and handle it well. There are times as a church planter where I just say, "This is insane." For me, admitting that I can't do it on my own and with my own abilities is a huge challenge. Trusting God's promises, remembering the cross, and surrendering to the will of God are the only ways to overcome that sense of escape and fear of failing.

How does deceit get in the way of your growth?

TONY. Deceit is countered with one word: *transparency*. I think there has to be a real transparency that shows your humanness. It is easy to say, "I was a _____," in the past tense. However, saying, "I am a_____," is a whole different story. Transparency is about the present, your ability to be honest about who you are, and how things are today. It is sharing with others who you really are and not pretending to be what you think they want you to be. I am learning to be transparent with my staff and leadership teams. I am finding that most of my fears revolve around what people think of me. And those fears tend to keep me from ever coming into the light of transparency, which will keep me from God's best.

What are some personal-growth recommendations for people like you?

BRAD. Find a mentor.

Having a mentor in my life who is willing to invest in

me personally by challenging and confronting areas of needed growth has been pivotal to my development. When I think back to times when spiritual growth has been the strongest, it has always been directly related to a mentor or close friend in my life. I believe life lessons are incredibly important. Seeing and understanding the contents of somebody else's life helps you discern the opportunities, challenges, and decisions in your own life. So I would say that finding a mentor is critical for a Jacob.

TONY. Practice humility.

There are three major things that I use in my attempt to cultivate humility in my life: prayer, the Word of God, and meditation. Talking to Him, being in His Word, hearing from Him, and really taking time to reflect on it. It becomes the foundation of humility. It's when we say, "You are God and I'm not. You have bigger plans than I could ever manufacture. Please allow me to walk and hear Your Spirit every step of the way. Speak to me and recall these Scriptures to mind the rest of my day." When we begin meditating on the spiritual dynamic in the morning, I think it reorients our focus from ourselves to Christ.

Also, recalibrate your focus.

The things that matter most are usually not the things you spend most of your time working so hard to accomplish. I was reminded of this recently when I overheard a conversation between my wife and our oldest son. My wife asked Ethan, "What does Mommy love doing most in the world?" Without hesitation, he said, "Read her Bible." Then, she asked, "What about Daddy? What does he love doing most in the world?" He said, "Working out with me in the gym"—which wasn't as spiritual as his mother, but at least he really believed I loved being with him.

Then my wife asked our two-and-a-half-year-old daughter, Peyton, "Hey, Peyton, what do you think Mommy loves to do most in this world?" She said back, "Oh, I don't know. Maybe Bible studies." Then she asked, "What about Daddy? What does Daddy love doing most in the world?" And with the same quick response, she said, "Be on his phone."

This spoke to me deeply, because children say what they see. My daughter saw what was most important to me. From her perspective, my phone and my work were number one. That broke my heart. We all have to recalibrate our focus on what's most important. We can't be so focused on our goal that we lose sight of the real goals in our lives.

Do you have any final thoughts for us?

BRAD. One of the phrases that my team and I are talking about these days is "messy moments of inconvenience." Sometimes God uses those messy moments that we may feel are inconvenient for the greatest results, for the greatest change, and for the greatest impact. If we are consumed by the busyness of life, we tend to miss these moments. As a Jacob personality, we are often too consumed by what's next (our next accomplishment, dream, or vision) that we miss "this" moment. God does His best work when we surrender to Him in *this* moment and trust His faithfulness for the moments to come.

TONY. Sometimes there can be a frustration with your current situation because you know where you are going to end up, and your dreams are so big that the present can seem so small. Don't forget that the spot you are in is the spot you are supposed to be in and the one God has called you to be in. Psalm 37:3 says, "Dwell in the land and cultivate faithfulness" (NASB).

If you can learn to do well what you are doing now, then you will eventually do what God has called you to do next. Work diligently where you are, learn to be teachable, and enjoy the spot you are in. The tendency as a Jacob is to strive for the next big thing—to be someone or do something. There seems to always be somewhere else you want to be. Hence, your life becomes a constant pursuit of what is to come.

Where you are is where you are. Trust God and let that be enough. Pour into what God has given you now. The tireless pursuit of the next thing can cause you to miss some of the best stuff in life: friendships, children, a relationship with your spouse, or a deep walk with God. At the end of your life, you don't want to look back at your life to see that you have accomplished so much but have left no real legacy.

Tony's Resource Recommendations

Edwards, Gene. *Tale of Three Kings.* Carol Stream, IL: Tyndale House, 1992.

Tozer, A.W. *The Pursuit of God.* Camp Hill, PA: Christian Publications, 1982.

Lewis, C. S. *Weight of Glory.* New York: HarperOne, 2001.

McManus, Erwin Raphael. *The Barbarian Way.* Nashville: Thomas Nelson, 2005.

Cymbala, Jim. *Fresh Wind, Fresh Fire.* Grand Rapids: Zondervan, 2003.

Brad's Resource Recommendations

Krzyzewski, Mike. *Leading with the Heart.* New York: Warner Business Books, 2001.

Kinnaman, David and Gabe Lyons. *UnChristian.* Grand Rapids: Baker, 2008.

Hybels, Bill. *Axiom.* Grand Rapids: Zondervan, 2011.

Nouwen, Henri J. M. *In the Name of Jesus.* New York: Crossroad, 1992.

Stanley, Andy. *Visioneering.* Sisters, OR: Multnomah Books, 1999.

Some Thoughts before Moving On

If you are like Jacob, here are some thoughts for you:

- The next time you take a vacation, don't work. Leave it all at home. Even though this statement may not naturally resonate with you, the most beneficial thing you can do right now is to take time to relax.

- Consider taking a nap this Saturday.

- Remember this truth: God loves you for who you are, not for what you do.

- List three things you really like to do besides work.

  1.

  2.

  3.

  Now schedule a time to do each one of these over the next six weeks.

- When you hear *deception*, it may be easy to think, *Hey, I'm not a liar!* But you are very good at keeping the "real you" hidden. So don't be afraid to get vulnerable with those close to you. Start by telling a trusted friend some things about you that you have never told him or her before.

Chapter 9

David

Mike Breaux

David was passionate, strong, creative, and loved. He was the king of Israel for forty years, and the Bible describes David as a man after God's own heart (1 Sam. 13:14). David was promised that the Savior of the world would be his descendant. David was a shepherd, musician, worshiper, and courageous warrior. He trusted in the sovereignty of God, evident by his decision to face a giant as a kid. He survived the chase of a mad king, defended his people against many nations, and prevailed against an attempted coup from one of his own sons. He wrote poems and songs of worship that fill the book of Psalms in the Bible. Despite lapses in his judgment and moral behavior, David pursued godliness and faithfulness throughout his life. He left a lasting legacy of bold faith and obedience.

ELEMENTS OF YOUR PERSONALITY

If you have a David personality, you are warm, compassionate, intuitive, and expressive. You love the stillness and quiet. Creativity is your lifeblood and you have the ability to feel things deeply. However, you can be plagued with self-doubt. You are motivated to search and to find your identity in order to express who you are and find meaning and significance. You surround yourself with things that you think are compelling and beautiful.

For you, to create is to live! Establishing a true, honest, and unique persona is important to you. Because you have the capacity to see what others miss, you sometimes feel out of the mainstream and mistakenly feel less competent socially. Sometimes this power to empathize and see the uncommon thread in things can lead you to see yourself as one of a kind.

The Best of You

You are abundantly and intuitively creative, expressing the personal and the universal, possibly in a work of art. You are inspired, self-renewing, and regenerating. You have an uncanny ability to turn ordinary life experiences into something profound and valuable. At your best, you are honest with yourself and those around you. You can address an issue, problem, or feeling without overreacting and without others feeling like you are being patronizing. You love to discover the truth in each experience. When you are at your best, you are looking for God and His creative power even in tough situations, conflicts, and mistakes. You are able to heighten reality through passionate feelings and imagination.

The Other Side of You

Harnessing your feelings can be hard for you and when you cannot control them, you are prone to blame and hold grudges. In these times, it is wise to trust God with your hurts and allow Him to make things right. Try to separate godly conviction from undue anger at yourself. Move toward right thinking and wise living by reading Psalms and Proverbs and refuse to get stuck in the past. If you become attached to longing and disappointment, you may not be able to recognize the many treasures in your life.

Primary Spiritual Inhibitor That Blocks Your Frequency: Envy

You have the tendency to become envious of another person's talent, success, good fortune, wealth, recognition, honor, or advantages. You can become preoccupied with a sense of discontent that is primarily based on what others have. Unlike covetousness or greed, envy is fundamentally comparative in nature.

Meet Someone Like You

Mike Breaux (and that is "Bro" not "Bree-Ox"). Mike is the teaching pastor at Heartland Community Church in Rockford, Illinois, and he also regularly teaches at Southland Christian Church in Lexington, Kentucky. He is the author of *Identity Theft* and *Making Ripples.*[1]

Tell us a little bit about your journey.

MIKE. I have been involved in ministry for a long, long time—since I was eighteen years old. I have been a student pastor and senior pastor, and I planted a church in Las Vegas, which was one of the greatest thrills of my life. I came back to Lexington, Kentucky, to lead a church that was in transition, and I was there for eight years. It was my hometown. To be in a culture that I knew growing up (a culture that is a lot of religion, but not a whole lot of talk of relationship with God) and be able to bring the experience of the grace of God from when I was in Vegas was pretty cool. We were able to see people from every walk of life coming to Christ. When I came back to Lexington, I challenged the church to say, "Okay, we need to extend grace to people who are far from God." There were challenges, but it was such a thrill for eight years.

Then I got a call from Willow Creek Community Church in Barrington, Illinois, to help transition some stuff they had going on there and teach regularly. I felt led to go do that, so I did. Heartland Community Church was using all the videotaped teachings from Willow Creek's weekend services at the time, so I inadvertently became the teaching pastor for a church about fifty miles away, with people I had never met. I would drive out to Rockford occasionally to teach and when I got there, people would ask, "Hey, how's Debbie? How are your kids?" I'd say, "What? I don't even know you people." It was kind of crazy. Five years later, I joined the teaching team at Heartland and have been doing that ever since. I love what I do.

What have you learned over the years about your spiritual growth?

MIKE. Through the years, it has been taught and presumed by many that, "If you want to grow spiritually, you have got to do this, this, and this." The ancient spiritual disciplines are great, but they don't fit everybody all the time. Take journaling, for example. For me, I will journal occasionally. When I take time to journal, I write, write, and write, pouring my heart out to God. But if I'm honest, it is not a daily practice for me and I think that's okay.

I have had pastors tell me I need to have a quiet time that's separate from the time I spend preparing sermons. I understand the intention behind that, but that doesn't really work for me. I try to have quiet time throughout the day as opposed to just in the morning, or just in the evening. It's the way my personality is wired. There are definitely moments throughout my day where I know it is just God and me. I have learned what resonates in my heart and what works for me. So when I am preparing for the weekend message, I am saying, "God, teach me. Speak to me here, so that I can internalize this. I want to teach other people what You have already taught me." That's been really helpful for me. For my personality, it does not help to separate the two. Don't feel guilty when you don't do exactly what other people say you should do to grow. Find what works for you, and then do it.

What can be a challenge?

MIKE. Everybody has valley experiences. Sometimes there are challenges that their specific personality helped them get into but that can also help them get out of it. I always find that I can get out of those valleys when I talk to someone about what I am going through—when I get in community with those who can help me. I think all of us can have a tendency to isolate ourselves when we experience pain. Bluntly stated, that's one of the worst things you could do. I have learned that if you are going through tough stuff, make sure you stay dialed into a circle of community and have friends who will pull you out. You will be surprised how many people have gone through a similar experience.

Peter and Judas are great examples of this idea. Both of these disciples betrayed Jesus and were emotionally torn up by their mistakes. However, what they did after the mistake and remorse made all the difference. Judas had remorse, but he isolated himself and ended up taking his own life. Peter had remorse, but the next time you see Peter, he is with a group of guys. He stayed in community, which probably saved his life.

How does envy get in the way of your growth?

MIKE. Envy reveals your self-centered nature, because it is about yourself. Envy is resenting God's goodness in somebody else's life, while ignoring His goodness in mine. Envy distracts you from the ways God has blessed your life. When you look at someone else's life, you find yourself saying, "I wish I had that. I wish I could do that. I wish I got that recognition."

Envy steals your gratitude and you start living a less grateful life, which leads you to a place of entitlement. You start thinking, *I deserve that* or *This or that should have happened.* A life lived with envy can take you down some pretty dark roads. I need to regularly remind myself that I do not want to go down that road.

I've been trying for years to live by Romans 12:15: "Rejoice with those who rejoice; mourn with those who mourn." I find it much harder to rejoice with those who rejoice than to mourn with those who mourn. That's part of envy. By the grace of

God, I think I have been doing pretty well in this area. Discovering this about myself has served as a great reminder of the dark path that envy can lead you down. It brings you to the center of the universe, and that's never a good place to be.

What are some recommendations for personal growth for people like you?

MIKE. First, remember who you are.

There is nothing more foundational than knowing who God is. He is your Father, your Abba, your Daddy, the Lover of your soul, and your Creator. You are a treasured child of His, and that's your identity. That's who you are. Until you know that, you will try to find all kinds of stuff to answer that question. When you discover who you are in Christ, it sweeps away all insecurity because you know who you are— you know you are accepted. You know that you are somebody.

When Paul wrote a letter to the church in Ephesus, he prayed that they would realize how wide, deep, high, and long God's love was for them (Eph. 3:18). He wanted them to grasp how deep God's love is for them. God wants the same for you. I have written a little bit about that word *grasp*. The root of that word means to decay or rust or eat all the way through. Paul was saying, "I don't want you to just know about God's love just in case you are trying to win a game of Bible Jeopardy. I want you to really grasp it and let it eat all the way through you."

Knowing who you are in Christ is the salvation that builds a great life. Without that, it is hard to grow spiritually. You would have too many insecurities in the way. If you don't know the love of God, you are going to live an insecure, anxious, fearful life. You won't be able to grow into the person God wants you to. I really do think it's the ballgame for spiritual growth.

Second, think new thoughts.

People like me are so introspective. I tend to live in my thoughts. That is why I always need to remind myself to renew my mind with the right kind of thoughts. It is the key to connecting with God on my frequency. I have learned that there are some things God will not do for me, and renewing my mind is one of those things. God's job is to transform me, but He does this when I am renewing my mind. As I renew my mind to a different way of thinking, God starts to transform me from the inside out.

I have a friend named Paul. He spent three years in prison for some choices he made before he knew Christ. During his time in jail, he began to understand how important it was to renew his mind. When he left prison, he started showing up at the church all the time. And I mean, all the time. I remember seeing Paul at the church for what seemed like the twentieth time that week, and I said to him, "You know, you don't have to be here this much." Paul fired back at me and said, "Yes, I do. For fifty-three years, I followed a certain way of thinking. My mind has certain ruts in it, and I've got to get some new ruts."

It's like a tractor in a field where there are deep ruts. Often, the person driving the tractor doesn't even need to steer; it just keeps following the ruts and it is difficult to turn. That is how it is with our mind. There isn't a DELETE button in our brain. We still have those old images and patterns of sin in our head. If we don't start to form new ruts, we will end up in the same old ruts of sin because that is what we know. I think that's why the identity thing is so important. When we start going down those old ruts again, God is saying, "That's not who you are anymore. It does not match up. That's the old one. That's the old life. Come on. Get back on the new path." That's one of the reminders that keeps me going in the direction God wants me to go. When I start to go back, I hear God say, "That's not who you are anymore."

Finally, live aware.

I wrote a life mission statement about twenty-five years ago that said, "I want to look, love, and live like Jesus." In order for me to look, love, and live like Jesus, I need to hang out with Jesus, read about Jesus, and study Jesus. So every year I spend a considerable amount of the year reading the Gospels. I try to pay attention to the way He lived and do my best to look, love, and live like Him. I cannot pull it off by myself. That's why surrender and a humble attitude are so huge. I get it wrong so much, but when I do, I feel the Holy Spirit reminding me, "Come on, man. That's not who you are anymore. You said you want to look, love, and live like Jesus. Come on."

The Holy Spirit is not just with you; He is in you. He is in you 24/7. That reality makes a huge difference in the way you approach life. People ask me how much time I spend with the Lord. I say, "All day." He is not going anywhere. He is with me all day. Because He is in me, there is a power, there is a reminder, there is a guide, and there is a teacher inside of me. It is life-changing and transformational. He is the one who moves in and does it from the inside out. Live in that awareness.

Do you have any final thoughts for us?

MIKE. You don't need to make this life any more complicated than it already is. Remember Micah 6:8, which says, "What does the LORD require of you? To act justly and to love mercy and to walk humbly with your God." So act justly—be like Him. Love mercy—live beyond yourself. And walk humbly with God. Isaiah 66:2 says, "These are the ones I look on with favor: those who are humble and contrite in spirit, and who tremble at my word." God says, "You know what I am impressed with? I am impressed with humble people." So this much I know: you are never going to grow into what God intended if you don't humble yourself. Humility is a soil in which all lives flourish.

I have also coached, taught, and mentored young pastors a lot. I tell all of them, "Be yourself. Don't try to be anybody else other than who you are. Talk the way you talk. Just be you." That's one of the things that I love about David. King Saul offered David armor that did not fit him before he killed Goliath. And David said, "No, that's not me." A lot of us, in that situation, would say, "Well, that's what you are supposed to wear." But David says, "No, that's not me. I am pretty good with a rock and a sling. I am a shepherd. I can do that."

I encourage everyone to be confident in the way God made them and to be themselves. Don't try to be anybody else. Be who God wired you to be and be content with that. Be the best you that you can be. Try to follow God's voice on a daily basis and take some risks. It's simple, but following God will take you down a path that you never thought you'd be able to go.

MIKE'S RESOURCE RECOMMENDATIONS

Manning, Brennan. *Abba's Child.* Colorado Springs: Nav-Press, 2002.

Ortberg, John. *The Life You've Always Wanted.* Grand Rapids: Zondervan, 2002.

Passion: Worship. Sixsteps Records, 2010. CD.

Miller, Donald. *A Million Miles in a Thousand Years*. Nashville: Thomas Nelson, 2009.

Forrest Gump. Paramount Pictures, 1994. DVD.

Some Thoughts before Moving On

If you are like David, here are some thoughts for you:

- Because you are a creative at heart, find ways to make some of the things you must do in your everyday life fun, creative, and playful.

- If the work you do for an income is not particularly creative, be sure to take regular portions of your free time for ideas that you need to formulate.

- It is very important for you to develop a good habit of sleep, eating, exercise, and work. Be disciplined in these four areas. They will make a huge difference in your life.

- Remind yourself of this truth: God has made you perfectly and has given you everything you need. You are capable and lovable—just as you are.

- You must address your tendency to be envious head-on! First, make a list of things that you are grateful for.

Write it big, then post that list where you see it every day. Next, list some things you admire in someone else around you. Over the next year, work to develop those same qualities in yourself.

Chapter 10

Luke

Mark Batterson

Luke was quiet, efficient, studious, and thorough. Luke lived at the same time as Jesus, was a companion of Paul, and is often credited as the primary author of the most detailed book of the Gospels. He had an eye for detail, sought evidence, and paid attention to the facts, leaving us valuable insights from Jesus' life and the beginning of the first church. Luke lived a life of dedication to the Lord. He was a well-educated physician and he loved applying his skills as a physician to the mission of reaching others for Christ. Luke recognized (with God's help and inspiration) that future generations would want to know about God's love and not just feel it. Luke tried to be open, careful, persistent, and correct in his work as a Christ-follower. He was a scribe and historian to some of the most important events of his day, and for that, we are all blessed.

ELEMENTS OF YOUR PERSONALITY

If you have a Luke personality, you are a person who values knowledge and acquiring expertise in a given subject area. Using your ability to observe and synthesize information, you meticulously analyze situations. Your objectivity serves you well, and you are able to resist following a crowd, if the crowd is going down the wrong path. Sensible and pragmatic, you tend to stay inside your thoughts rather than show your heart openly to everyone. You are careful about who you choose to trust and you enjoy a few deep friendships over many shallow ones. You love to figure out why people, places, and things are the way they are. You want to understand how things work. You are always asking questions, thinking about problems, and looking for solutions. Because you are analytical, some people may call you "stoic." You like to think of it as "rational." You fear any situation that will cause you to be inaccurate about a given subject and, therefore, be seen as less than competent. You also tend to overthink situations, which can lead to a loss of productivity.

The Best of You

Ideas and innovations fascinate you. You love a good, fair argument that is based on facts and analytical reasoning. You see potential where others fail to see it and you enjoy being on the cutting edge. Independent and looking for answers to mysteries, you consider all the possibilities. You have a keen eye for detail and you are able to convey a sense of understanding to people.

The Other Side of You

Deep down, you may have a sinking feeling that you do not have the ability to do things as well as they should be done. Sometimes the idea of "not measuring up" causes you to withdraw to the place you feel safest—your mind. It is easy for you to pull away from people when you feel threatened, and you can stay in isolation for too long. You are comfortable being alone, but sometimes you distance yourself from authentic community.

The Primary Spiritual Inhibitor That Blocks Your Frequency: Pride of Knowledge

You have a tendency to place a high value on what you know and then "power up" on people who know less about a certain topic. While you love knowledge and studying, you may be tempted to study so that you can be better prepared for the next debate. What you've read and what you know can become increasingly important to your feeling of significance.

MEET SOMEONE LIKE YOU

Mark Batterson. Mark is the lead pastor at National Community Church in Washington, D.C., and author of several books including *In a Pit with a Lion on a Snowy Day, Circle Maker,* and *Primal.*[1]

What are you doing these days?

MARK. I'm the lead pastor of National Community Church in Washington, D.C. We are one church with seven locations with about two-thirds of our church being singles and twenty-somethings. So we are very young and a very transient congregation with about 40 percent turnover every year because of our where we are in the country. We have an immediate family of a couple thousand people who attend on any given weekend and then we have an extended family who have been a part of NCC but have moved to other parts of the country or other parts of the world.

Why is growth important?

MARK. One of the big lessons I learned early on is that it is really easy to overestimate what you can accomplish in one year and at the same time underestimate what you can accomplish in ten years. As it pertains to pastoring, I have tried to take the long view. My father-in-law planted and then pastored a church for more than thirty years. That inspires me. I started young enough at NCC, so I have a good shot of getting forty or fifty years there. I really get excited about what God could do in the nation's capital over that time frame.

On a personal level, I've never worried that much about church growth. I've always worried about personal growth. I feel like my greatest debt to our congregation is that I am growing personally and spiritually. If I am not growing, then I am not leading them well by example.

What has helped you grow spiritually?

MARK. I love to read. I remember hearing that the average author takes two years to write a book. So when I read a book, I feel like I am getting two years of life experience. If I do the math correctly, reading one hundred books in the next few years would be like gaining two hundred years of experience. That being said, I think reading is such a key way to continuing to grow, expand, and stretch your mind.

Also, I came up with this formula a few years ago that I've seen to be true in my life. "A change in pace plus a change in place equals a change of perspective." If I am feeling stuck in my spiritual growth, I always consider changing my pace or my place and it usually helps change my perspective. Interrupting my routine is usually a great way for me to experience some personal growth when I'm plateaued. Routines aren't bad; actually, they can be very helpful when it comes to your spiritual growth. But if those routines become just a routine instead of being things that truly stretch your mind and heart, then you may need to disrupt those routines or change them.

For example, I have tried to read different translations of the Bible or tried fasting around the New Year or around Pentecost. Mixing it up can go a long way in your spiritual growth.

What advice would you give people who are similar to you?

MARK. Channel your personality and your drive in the right way. Sometimes I find myself reading the Bible with the only intention being to prepare a sermon. People who love knowledge usually love to teach, but they must be careful to allow the truth to also speak to them. Instead of reading the Bible like a teacher, I need to invite God to speak to me in a more personal way, where I am really trying to grow in my relationship with the Lord. One of the ways I have done that has been a one-year Bible. It has helped me stay on track spiritually. Daily reading that is outlined for you is almost like having a workout program that has been tailored for you. You have a schedule that you can follow.

Also, it's important to know which season you are in at the time. In January, I am naturally the most motivated person on the planet. I am a New Year's person—fresh start, new goals, and a whole new year ahead of me. But sometimes during the summer I can lose a little bit of motivation and a lot of focus. When I lose motivation and focus, I drift a little bit spiritually. I'm trying to put a few things in place this summer that will help me guard against that drift. Before going on vacation or sabbatical, I've taken the time to select portions of Scripture and several books that I know I am going to read in order to keep me headed in the right direction. Being aware of those seasons when I tend to fade spiritually helps me put some structures in place to prevent it.

What is the biggest challenge for you?

MARK. The biggest challenge I face is the lack of margin. There is just not enough margin in my life. In some ways, that can be good because a lack of margin can keep you out of trouble. But sometimes a lack of margin can get you in trouble if you aren't using that margin in the right way.

Paul makes a statement in Scripture about how all things are permissible, but not all things are beneficial (1 Cor. 10:23). I think many Christians live to a level of permissibility but don't pay enough attention to what is beneficial. In other words, we don't pay attention to the things that are "best." I have found it helpful to ask myself, "What in my life is permissible but isn't necessarily beneficial?" One of the things that we are doing as a family is turning off the TV for June, July, and August. We canceled our DirectTV because we wanted to experiment with three months of no television. Why? Well, it's amazing how much margin comes back into our lives when you can't sit down and vegetate in front of the television. It's just an experiment, and if it helps create more margin for God in our lives, then it was worth it.

How does community affect our spiritual growth?

MARK. There are intrapersonal processors and interpersonal processors. In other words, I think there are people who are best at processing decisions and information by themselves—in their own mind and heart. But there are a lot of other people who are interpersonal processers. They love being in brainstorming sessions with others and an environment where they can process decisions with several people.

Too often, we don't recognize what type of processor we are and then we get frustrated because we can't do what we think we should be able to do. Acknowledging the way you are naturally wired to connect in community can set you free and help you understand the way God created you to grow in community.

How do you encourage people at National Community Church to grow?

MARK. One of our core values at NCC is that everything is an experiment. We take an experimental approach to absolutely everything we do. It's a wonderful way to approach discipleship, too, because you can't fail. You may find things that don't suit your personality or don't work for you, but as long as you continue to experiment, you will find some things that do work. I think that when you stop experimenting, you stop growing.

Do you have any final thoughts for us?

MARK. I have learned that after fifteen years of pastoring, there is nothing worse than doing ministry with an empty soul. And there is nothing greater than doing ministry out of the fullness of what God is doing in your heart. So when it comes down to how you are doing personally and spiritually, it has a great effect on your ability to help others.

There are some amazing things happening at NCC right now and we are experiencing unprecedented favor in the D.C. area. In the midst of that, I have been sensing a mantra in my spirit. It's simply this: "Stay humble, stay hungry." I have heard it in my mind and heart probably a thousand times. I hear it over and over: "Stay humble, stay hungry." When God blesses you, you have two paths you can go. It is either going to turn into praise or turn into pride. There is no in-between. God opposes the proud. I have also leaned on 1 Corinthians 8:2, which says, "Those who think they know something do not yet know as they ought to know." That keeps me humble. The more I know, the more I know how much I don't know. So I think as a leader and as a disciple, you need to stay humble. The best way to stay humble is to stay in a posture of prayer, either physically or spiritually on your knees.

The other piece is to stay hungry. If someone said, "Mark, if I could give you one thing. I'll do one thing for you. One wish granted." For me and for our congregation, my request would be to ask for spiritual hunger. How hungry are you spiritually? Are you dying to self? Are you allowing Christ to be formed in you? Try repeating these words in your mind and heart: "Stay humble, stay hungry."

MARK'S RESOURCE RECOMMENDATIONS

Heath, Dan and Chip Heath. *Switch.* New York: Broadway Books, 2010.

Ramsey, Dave. *EntreLeadership.* New York: Howard, 2011.

Collins, Jim. *Great by Choice.* New York: HarperCollins, 2011.

Kinnaman, David. *You Lost Me.* Grand Rapids: Baker, 2011.

SOME THOUGHTS BEFORE MOVING ON

If you are like Luke, here are some suggestions for you:

- This week, try putting yourself in a setting where you are not an expert. Speak up and interact, even if you end up saying something that will make you look foolish.

- With those who are close to you, take a risk and listen. Don't try to fix anything. Avoid the urge you may have to prove that you know something. Just listen.

- Being alone is natural for you. But remember that interactive experiences with others are key to deepening your understanding.

146

- Optimism may not come naturally for you. Learn to see things through a lens of optimism. Choose to believe the best about other people's actions and about your situation.

- Don't let your knowledge cause you to "puff up" and become prideful (1 Cor. 8:1). If you are not careful, you can come across as a know-it-all. Ask good questions about things you don't know about and let someone else be the expert once in a while.

Chapter 11

Timothy

Jon Acuff

Timothy was committed, loyal, and enthusiastic. At the time when he met the apostle Paul, it was clear that anyone who signed up to be an ambassador for Christ would not have an easy life. Timothy knew about the persecution Paul had faced and was facing, yet he chose to join him anyway. Timothy's faith in God, love and loyalty to Jesus, and commitment to the fiery apostle Paul helped him overcome the fear that may have gripped him. Timothy traveled with Paul as a young man and then spent fifteen years leading the church of Ephesus. He devoted himself to the mission of preaching the message of Jesus. Even though Timothy may have felt afraid and inadequate to complete the task, he remained loyal and faithful at heart and, as a result, God used him to advance His kingdom.

ELEMENTS OF YOUR PERSONALITY

If you have a Timothy personality, you have the desire to attach yourself to a worthy cause and defend it to the very end. You will defend your faith and you may be more likely to stand up for an idea that you believe in than to stand up for yourself. You are smart and witty, but you sometimes worry that you are being too intense. People might tell you to lighten up, but your commitment to what is right is serious business.

As a friend, you are steadfast, responsible, and warm. You have good discernment about people and activities, generally leading others into right choices. Sometimes you feel that you are able to carry the weight of responsibility better than others. In quiet moments, you worry about being left alone to fend for yourself. Because you don't like to appear needy, you are sometimes left with no support. Risk-taking is not your first choice and you prefer things to be safe and stable. You hate feeling helpless or worried, so you tend to go with what you know is secure.

The Best of You

Once you have given your heart and mind to someone or something, it sticks. What you say and what you do are congruent, which makes other people trust you. Your dependability is your strength. You are willing to pay the price for your beliefs. You don't give up easily and enjoy persevering to the end.

The Other Side of You

You sometimes struggle with self-confidence. You have a hard time transitioning your strong belief in others toward yourself. When you are unsure, you can choose to procrastinate, blame others for what is making you anxious, or worry about something you cannot control. At times, you can interfere with your own success because of low self-confidence. You tend to get edgy and testy when you are upset or angry, which is confusing for those who perceive you as positive and solution oriented.

The Primary Spiritual Inhibitor That Blocks Your Frequency: Anxiety/Fear

You have the tendency to experience a feeling of worry, nervousness, or unease about an imminent event or something with an uncertain outcome. You may feel overwhelmed or burdened for no apparent reason. You are attracted to situations in which you can control the outcome. Stress is normal to you, and you find it difficult to trust God when there is not a clear solution to a problem.

MEET SOMEONE LIKE YOU

Jon Acuff. Jon is an author of three books and blogger at stuff christianslike.net and jonacuff.com. His most recent book is called *Quitter.*[1]

How did you get started as a writer?

JON. I grew up in the church and it always weirded me out that sometimes, we as Christians don't use our best creativity to celebrate the One who we believe to be the Creator of creativity. Instead, we take a popular secular idea and sprinkle it with some God flavor and then take it as a church idea. So "Got Milk?" becomes "Got God?" Adidas becomes "Add Jesus." Burger King becomes "King of Kings."

When the website Stuff White People Like came along and it blew up (which was a satire about Caucasia, if you will), I thought, "What if I talked about that problem by being guilty of committing that problem?" So I started a Christian version of that website called Stuff White Christians Like, and the very first post was "Why do we like to rip off popular secular culture?" I thought I would write about it for a week and get bored with it, like all the other websites I have registered. But on day nine, four thousand people from around the world showed up. Since then 2.5 million people have read it. And it has been a really fun ride.

How was your experience taking the Monvee assessment?

JON. When I took the Monvee assessment, got my results, and read them, I was surprised how much it nailed me when it said, "You love to engage. You prefer to put something together instead of read the manual. You hate to sit on the sideline." That is completely and totally me. I want to jump in and get started. It also said, "You hate feeling helpless or worried. You tend to go with what feels secure," which is also dead-on. And "you can even at times interfere with your own success because of low self-confidence." That is true, without a doubt.

Was there anything about the assessment that surprised you?

JON. I am in a very big season right now, which is such a Christian phrase, but nonetheless, I'm in a season. I'm realizing that the one-size-fits-all approach with God does not fit and does not work. For years, I have framed my relationship with God by thirty minutes of quiet time. I would even set a timer. I'd write in the same journal, read the Bible, and do a few other things, all within that thirty minutes. He became a voodoo God for me. I had to do these specific practices in the right way and in the right sequence and that would make God happy with me.

If you were to ask me before the Monvee assessment, "Do you really engage with God through nature?" I would have said, "No, I don't." I really hate granola bars. So the line about needing to spend large chunks of time outdoors didn't seem to fit me at that moment. But I went to the beach recently, and I just let myself off the hook and tried to relax. I tend to be an idea guy, so in the past I tried to get caught up in all sorts of ideas on vacation. I would reason, "Well, I love generating ideas, so this is how I relax." It was a huge lie. I needed to truly empty myself to refuel. When I did that, an unmistakable peace overtook me.

Then I noticed something at the end of the vacation. About 70 percent of the pictures on my phone were of beautiful sunsets. And I realized that I totally connect with God through creation. So now that I have the permission of "you need to try to do this and that's okay," I feel free. Not "Did you journal today?" or "Wow, didn't spend time with God, did ya?" Now that I know that it's okay to connect with God through creation, there is freedom in that.

Sometimes I think we have the hardest time being students of ourselves. The enemy loves for us to forget about the things that make us happy and connect us with God. When I was talking with my wife about the assessment results, she said, "Of course that is the way you are. Look at your phone and all the photos of the sunset." I just had never seen that in myself.

How have you seen fear block your frequency?

Jon. Without a doubt, fear is something I have struggled with for years. Recently, I've started going through a list of statements every morning to help me address my fears. One example is, "Today is a gift from God, not a test." It changes the filter through which I experience my day. Often I'll write it down, think about it, pray about it, and carry it with me.

How do you address fear in your life?

JON. Having someone I can talk to about my fears has been extremely helpful. There's a guy I have breakfast with every other week and he works at a church close to where I live. He is just a super-creative guy with a ton of interests similar to mine. He calls me or I call him and he'll say, "Hey, here is what is going on." Or I'll call him and say, "I just went to this crazy good breakout at this conference and it has me all stressed. I'm horrible compared to that guy and I'm up next." He will help me think through it and we can talk about it. I'll say things to him that I have kept quiet about for years because I felt like I had to figure them out or I didn't want to be embarrassed. I didn't want someone to know I had a worry about something. Now that I am able to share my fears and worries, I have someone who reflects the truth back to me.

My fears and my thoughts and my anxieties aren't burglars that broke into my house without my welcome. They are often invited guests. I've realized that I can tell them to leave. I don't have to be a prisoner. This is not a home invasion. I get to choose my thoughts.

What are some personal-growth recommendations for people like you?

JON. First, fear is not a friend.

Don't think of worry and fear as a friend, but think of them as a foe. A friend of mine once challenged me about the voices in my head that I allow to influence my perspective. One of the voices that I have heard for years is, "Are you happy?" When I hear that voice consistently, I start to think, *Well, I am happy most of the time, but sometimes I am sad. Wait, why would I be sad? I have my dream job right now writing books and speaking full-time. If I'm not happy now, when will I ever be happy? Wow, I haven't thought about that. That kind of makes me unhappy. Maybe there is something that you can do that makes you perfectly happy. That's a lot of pressure. I feel unhappy.* It can become a never-ending downward spiral. There have been times when I thought that the downward spiral of fear and anxiety was a friend. I needed to realize that fear is not a friend. It is a foe.

One of my friends once said to me, "It's great that all these great things are happening in your life and you are becoming successful, but be careful not to get cocky. Hold on to that healthy sense of paranoia." And I said, "Stop! That can't be the only two options I have. And is there a healthy sense of paranoia?"

I frequently find myself getting caught up in the mentality

that my only two options are to either become a cocky jerk or hold on to a sense of paranoia. I don't buy that anymore. There has to be a middle ground where I can have humility, joy, and confidence and not just two polar extremes (a cocky jerk who sinks his own ship through his massive ego or a person who is overcome with fear and doubt). Fear is not my friend, and it is not yours either.

The Monvee assessment talked about how people like Timothy have a fear of starting things. That is totally true with me. I care about what I'm doing so much that I'm often afraid that it won't be perfect, even if I've never done it before. I had a counselor once tell me that a narcissist is someone who believes they will be amazing at things that they have never done before. Don't go there. Give yourself permission to be horrible at something. Otherwise, fear will become your friend.

Second, give yourself permission to grow.

I think we can sometimes put some conditions on growth. We think, *If I do A plus B plus C, God will be happy and growth will happen.* I just don't think it works that way. I have discovered that there is power in permission. For me, I've gotten the permission to engage with God through nature. *Wow, that counts?* I'm convinced the enemy loves to put the idea of "That doesn't count" in our heads. We think, *It doesn't count unless you read a certain amount of chapters. It doesn't count unless . . . [you fill in the blank].*

When I learned that I connect with God through nature, it was a powerful permission. It was okay that I didn't feel close to God by journaling. I heard John Ortberg once say, "Jesus never journaled." Give yourself permission to grow in the way God created you. Don't be so afraid to mess it up.

Finally, perfection is not required to grow.

Being a perfectionist is often seen as a good quality at first. People say, "Wow, what a hard worker! They are really taking care of things and doing it so well." However, I have learned that too much perfectionism leads to burnout; it leads you to a place where you become a shell.

How do I overcome that when it comes to my spiritual growth? Sometimes I have to remind myself that the decisions I make today aren't necessarily forever. A little trial and error is okay. Often I can get so paralyzed by the thought that I will make one misstep that will compromise my whole future. Some decisions could jeopardize my future, but let's be honest: sometimes people who are naturally worriers feel like every decision holds the world in the balance. We start to feel overwhelmed and burdened for no apparent reason. This stops the possibility for growth in our life. We should all want to do our absolute best to honor God with every part of our life, but there is grace and forgiveness when we mess up. Amazing grace that Jesus affords us through the cross.

Do you have any final thoughts for us?

JON. Don't underestimate how much your life will be impacted by your thoughts. Your thoughts will profoundly shape your days, weeks, and, ultimately, your life. In the past, I have seen my thoughts as separate, unconnected elements in my life. As I've grown, I have begun to see how my thoughts and my life are interconnected. My thoughts can blow up my day if I'm not careful. They can blow it up in beautiful fireworks of healthy, hopeful, God-inspired, God-breathed thoughts or blow it up like a bomb, destroying everything. When I let myself hold onto a thought of doubt, fear, anxiety, or obsession, it's dangerous. So that would be the first thing I would say: put some focus on your thoughts.

One other thing—it's not one-size-fits-all. Sometimes you may feel that whatever you are doing to grow does not count. For me, I tried to fit God in a certain size box. Things didn't come naturally, but I felt it was the only way I could connect with God. So I kept trying it and I kept not enjoying it. Until eventually I thought, "I don't enjoy spending time with God. I don't want to do this anymore." Then I realized that He has created me in a unique way to engage with Him. He has created you that way too. The more we can engage with Him in that way and turn to Him to understand the way that we grow, the better off we will be.

JON'S RESOURCE RECOMMENDATIONS

Miller, Donald. *Blue Like Jazz*. Nashville: Thomas Nelson, 2003.

Merton, Thomas. *The Wisdom of the Desert*. New York: New Directions, 1970.

MacDonald, Gordon. *Ordering Your Private World*. Nashville, Thomas Nelson, 1984.

Allgather.org by Mark Acuff

SOME THOUGHTS BEFORE MOVING ON

If you are like Timothy, here are some suggestions for you:

- This month, take some time to notice the uplifting and positive things people say about you. When you hear those things, write them down in a place where you can review them when you are feeling low.

- Remember that every thought has a positive or a negative charge. If you linger on fearful thoughts, it will lead to more fearful thoughts. Learn to recognize negative thoughts and release them.

- Life is not always certain. Sometimes things are left in limbo. Learning to accept that fact will help with your tendency to be anxious. Remember that the uncertainty will not last forever.

- List all the verses in the Bible that start with the phrase "fear not" or "don't be afraid" on index cards. Put them in a place where you will see them regularly.

Chapter 12

Solomon

Shauna Niequist

Solomon was wise, inventive, intelligent, and successful. He built beautiful gardens and structures, and he was chosen by God to build the temple. Solomon brought a level of peace, fame, and enjoyment to his people through serving God and honoring his birthright as the son of David. God offered Solomon the opportunity to be granted one wish for anything he wanted, and Solomon chose wisdom. The wisdom he received from God gave him wealth and power beyond comprehension. Solomon served as a king and righteous judge. The limitless possibilities available to him eventually caused him to become a person of excess. His explorative appetite for the unusual led him down some flawed paths. At one point, he opened himself to the worship of false gods. However, Solomon wrote a multitude of principles found in the Bible and concluded that at the end of the day, nothing is more important than knowing God. He left a great legacy of beauty, wisdom, and creativity.

ELEMENTS OF YOUR PERSONALITY

If you have a Solomon personality, you are playful, optimistic, and ready for anything. When you combine that with your practical versatility, you are unstoppable. Curiosity may have killed the cat, but it has led you into many fine adventures. Your greatest fears are related to boredom and insignificance. Pain, of any kind, is something you seek to avoid. You seek satisfaction both on the physical and emotional levels. In order to pursue your many dreams, you seek to acquire and maintain your freedom. You can be resistant to constraints, even those that sometimes may be good for you. Naturally curious and analytical, you find yourself in places of new impressions, whether at work or recreation. You love to make it up as you go. While you are not against a good plan, you don't want the plan to get in the way of living. You don't consider yourself to be intellectual or studious, but you are able to absorb information quickly and you are a fast learner.

The Best of You

You have a deep ability to experience and express gratitude. This allows you to feel humbled by the gift of life and experience a lot of joy through simple things. People like to be around you and you like to be around people. Because of your resilient personality, you are able to let go of relational hurt easily and move on. You love the phrase, "Forgive and forget" because there is too much life to explore to be stuck in the past.

The Other Side of You

Sometimes you are involved in so many interesting things that you have not mastered any of them. You can experience difficulties in the process of determining which of your interests you should dive deeper into with greater discipline. You can't seem to land on what you were made to do because you seem well suited for a variety of things. Increased activity can lead to stress and anxiety in your life, manifesting itself in busyness. You find ways to occupy your time and mind so you don't have to think about whatever it is that is bothering you. While most of the time these distractions are actually things you enjoy doing, they can keep you from dealing with real issues.

The Primary Spiritual Inhibitor That Blocks Your Frequency: Excess/Greed

You tend to have an insatiable appetite for more. It seems impossible, at times, to feel content and grateful with what you currently have or possess. The adage "The grass is always greener on the other side" can be your normal mode of operation. The desire for more money, opportunity, or power is the most likely pitfall for you. Be on guard against an insatiable desire to possess or acquire something, beyond what you need or deserve.

MEET SOMEONE LIKE YOU

Shauna Niequist. Shauna is the author of two books, *Cold Tangerines* and *Bittersweet,*[1] and blogs regularly at shauna niequist.com.

Tell us about what you are working on.

SHAUNA. I'm working on a third book called *Bread and Wine.* It's a collection of essays about life around the table. I'm discovering that God works most consistently in my life when I am spending time with the people I love around a table. When I slow down and dedicate myself to feeding them and listening to them, it ends up being nourishing both for them and for me. I'm really excited about this next project—I get to do a lot of cooking and entertaining and call it research for a book.

What stood out to you in your Monvee Discovery Summary?

SHAUNA. When the summary said, "You have the tendency to have an insatiable appetite for more," I completely agreed. Anyone who knows me well would say that is absolutely true. As I have grown as a Christian, as a woman, as a mother, and as an individual, I've realized that my insatiable approach to life can be a very beautiful thing. Exploring those appetites has allowed me to take risks, follow God's voice, and learn so much about life. But it can also be very destructive.

That's why the phrase "quality over quantity" really stuck out to me as well. I almost always choose quantity. I want to go more, play more, do more, schedule more, eat more, and buy more. My husband has said to me, "Sometimes just watching you is exhausting." When I allow more space and silence in my life, I'm able to experience the things I love on a much deeper level. "Quality over quantity" is definitely a key phrase that has been important to me for a long time.

What about your personality makes connecting with God easy for you?

SHAUNA. I think when someone of my personality type is doing well, there is a natural optimism, positivity, and sense of abundance that becomes evident in his or her life. When I'm doing well, it's easy for me to see God's fingerprints on everything and to realize that the world is a really beautiful place. The things that He created for us to enjoy are amazing gifts. When I take care of myself, gratitude comes very naturally.

However, on the flip side of that, the desire to experience the goodness in life can drive people like me to have a desire to experience everything on an excessive level. I'll think, *This tastes so good. Why not have more? If a little ice cream is great, why not have tons of ice cream? Watching the sunset is beautiful, why not stay up all night and look at the stars?* This tendency comes from a natural desire to enjoy life and can lead to a real spiritual sense of gratitude, but I need to be careful not to get excessive.

What can be a challenge for someone with this personality type?

SHAUNA. It may sound crazy, but I've learned I have a totally unrealistic view of both my time and my energy. When Aaron and I first started dating, he referred to it as the "Shauna Forty-Five." The "Shauna Forty-Five" stood for the forty-five minutes that I was habitually late for anything that I committed to. I had no idea how long things would actually take, so I was always late.

I have a friend who has the same personality type as me. Recently, there was a situation where we all paid for his inability to manage his schedule and be on time. He got too busy, committed to too many things, said yes to too many people, was overly optimistic, and then the whole thing crashed. As a result of his overcommitment, we all had to change our plans. And I realized in that moment that I have done that a thousand times, and the havoc it can wreak on other people is real. It can wear people out and make people frustrated when you don't come through. It's really helpful for me to be around people who are a lot like me, because it forces me to deal with the frustrating parts of my own personality.

How does excess get in the way of your growth?

SHAUNA. We are generally guided by a belief that more is more—that more is better. We believe that more will make us happy and fill up the emptiness inside us. We tend to hear the phrase "less is more," and we think, *Yeah, that's not for me. That's for other people.* But the richest seasons of my life have come when I have practiced the belief that less is more and that quality matters more than quantity.

It can be scary for someone of my personality type to choose less or to say no to something. There is this scarcity mentality that creeps in. I'll think, *If I don't eat this piece of cake now, I'll never have good cake again. If I don't go to the beach right now, I'll miss something there that will never happen again.* To practice the belief that there will be more down the road can really be transforming. There's only so much you can fit into a twenty-four-hour period, and I've ruined a lot of twenty-four-hour periods, hoping that I could cram everything I desire into that box. Quality is really better than quantity. Saying no is almost always a healthy choice for me.

What are some personal-growth recommendations for people like you?

SHAUNA. First, learn to listen to those around you.

God works most clearly in my life through prayer and community. Spending time in close-up, unvarnished, and intimate ways with friends I love is critical for my spiritual growth.

I had five friends come up and visit us at the lake recently—five girlfriends and seven kids! The way you live together during a week like that is very, very intimate. You're holding each other's kids and you're picking up after each other. One of my friends is a new mom, adjusting to motherhood, so there were some tears, and I love that really intimate part of friendship. I have very little energy or capacity for a cocktail party where the main conversation is, "Who are you? What do you do?" I am more of a "tell me your secrets, cry in front of me, let me help you, and let me see you without your makeup on" type of person.

The intimacy of an unvarnished life is really valuable to me. My spiritual life mostly happens in the context of a community of people I love, who love me, are willing to tell me the hard truth, and are willing to demonstrate their unvarnished life.

Second, understand and appreciate the uniqueness of others.

For my husband and me, understanding our personality

types has become really important for us. It's unlocked a lot of great conversations and helped us understand each other. Some marriages are based on similarities and some are based on opposites, and Aaron and I are definitely a marriage of opposites. I am very much an extrovert and he is very much an introvert. I like things to be fast-paced, moving all the time, and I tend to be an optimist. He prefers a small, quiet, and close-knit group of friends. He likes to be home a lot. He likes a lot of time to process things, and he prefers to work alone. We work best in our marriage when we honor the differences instead of trying to change the other person, because that never works.

When we were engaged or dating, I'm sure we both thought, "Pretty soon he or she will be just like me." Everybody who is married knows that you may try that for a while, but then you realize that it is never going to happen. It's not honoring to the way God made that person. The best thing we have learned is how to appreciate our differences and allow those differences to bring out the best in each other.

Finally, know the limits, but take opportunities.

Two important things that my parents gave me as a kid were very clear limits and lots of opportunities. I love being thrown into new situations, I love being challenged, and I love to travel. Because my parents knew this about me, my dad took me all over the world with him when I was young.

He would give me the job of checking us in at the gate, figuring out the train in Madrid, or figuring out what hotel to stay at in Paris. For me, that made life feel so exciting. As a pastor's kid, the church was never a terrible place that took my dad away. It was the exciting place that I got to go to with him. I went to fun meetings, got to travel, and got to see the world because of it. The church unlocked so many doors for me to experience things I would have never experienced. I'm really thankful that my parents watched me and knew how important those opportunities were to me.

The other thing that my parents gave me was the concept of limits. I was the classic strong-willed child. Every time my son, who is also a very strong-willed child, does something particularly naughty, my parents look at me and say, "We have prayed for thirty years that you would have a son this naughty. Don't think this is an accident. You deserve every bit of this." They're joking, mostly, but I am getting a taste of my own medicine.

My parents were very strict with me, particularly when I was young. They had firm expectations for me when it came to being kind, being patient, accepting limits, being told no, not talking back, managing my frustration, or managing my emotions. Now that I have a four-year-old, I really appreciate how hard it was for them to do that. It's so difficult as a parent to say no, again and again. It would be so much easier to say, "Oh, fine, I'll just give you whatever it is you want." My parents' careful parenting taught me to manage my strengths in a way that would be helpful to me, instead of letting me use my strengths in a way that would be destructive.

Do you have any final thoughts for us?

SHAUNA. As difficult as it is, saying no is almost always a healthy choice for me. When I do less, promise less, commit to less, try to juggle less, I'm more able to appreciate life's goodness. In an effort to experience everything, I get moving so fast that I really end up experiencing nothing—I get going so fast that I eat without tasting, sleep without dreaming, speak without listening, and drive without noticing anything but the destination. That's not how I want to live. Say no more often than you want to. Practice believing that less really is more. Choose quality over quantity as often as you can. You'll find that when you live more slowly and intentionally, the beauty and depth you're looking for are so much more apparent than when you're chasing them full speed.

SHAUNA'S RESOURCE RECOMMENDATIONS

Lamott, Anne. *Traveling Mercies.* New York: Anchor, 1999.

Rohr, Richard. *Everything Belongs.* New York: Crossroad, 2003.

Foster, Richard. *Celebration of Discipline.* New York: Harper-Collins, 1998.

Cloud, Henry. *Integrity.* New York: HarperCollins, 2006.

Some Thoughts before Moving On

If you are like Solomon, here are some suggestions for you:

- Learn to be grateful for what you have instead of fixating on what you want. It is a spiritual discipline for you. When you find yourself in the rush of what you want, stop and practice dwelling on all that you have already received.

- You are often described as an optimist, but there is a place for recognizing the reality of a situation. Problems won't always just go away. Sometimes you will need to address the issue head-on. Be careful in how you approach conflict, using the process in Matthew 18 as a guide.

- This month, spend time doing a Bible study on contentment. It will help you remember that you have all you need in Him.

- One great way to deal with greed or the need for more is by practicing quality over quantity. This month, instead of doing more, focus on what is right in front of you. This month's mantra for you is "quality, quality, quality."

Chapter 13

Samson

Karl Clauson

Samson was strong, resilient, smart, and brave. He had greater-than-average physical strength. He tore apart a lion that attacked him, killed dozens of Philistines with a jawbone, and knocked down a structure with his arms. Outraged by the domination of his people by foreigners, he sought to make the situation right at great personal cost. Samson was brave and courageous; however, he was often brash and reckless. His success brought encouragement and deliverance for many people. Unfortunately, Samson acted alone much of the time and eventually became vulnerable to temptation. Giving in to temptation caused him to be deceived by a woman, robbed of his strength, humiliated by his enemy, and enslaved to the grinding of grain. In the end, God redeemed Samson's humiliation and gave him the final victory over his adversaries.

ELEMENTS OF YOUR PERSONALITY

If you have a Samson personality, you are dynamic, resourceful, strong, and persistent. People appreciate your strength and self-confidence, especially in a crisis. As a natural leader, you are decisive, practical, and protective. You seek to control your circumstances and surroundings and people respond to your direction.

You value self-reliance and avoid appearing weak or vulnerable in front of others. You strive to maintain control of your life. Self-preservation and protection are two of your key motivators. You expect others to appreciate your efforts and assume that they should show that through their cooperation with your plans. You fear rejection and you tend to protect the side of you that, surprisingly to others, can be easily hurt.

You love taking charge of a situation and meeting any challenge. You fight for what you believe is right and will not tolerate feeling used by someone for his or her gain. You pride yourself on being honest and direct, and some would say you confront people easily and effectively. You have always had a great deal of willpower, which makes tough decisions seem to come easy to you.

The Best of You

You are indignant and discontent with injustice. Therefore, you use your strength to defend those who are weak or can't act on their own behalf. Your strong work ethic is inspiring to people who see you tackle large issues that intimidate others, and you frequently seek creative solutions to old problems. You are compassionate and seek to honor those you love. You are very aware of what people think of you, but you usually don't let that get in the way of doing and saying what you believe in. You love to promote people, to provide for others, and to provide opportunities.

The Other Side of You

God has wired you with resilience and independence, but this can also be something that causes problems for you because you can be careless for your body, mind, or soul. The urgency of the present can encourage you to sacrifice the future in terms of health and relationships. Your high energy level can sometimes cause you to set unrealistic expectations for your followers. They, in turn, may choose to stop following or continue to follow at an unreasonable cost to themselves.

Because you hide vulnerability, others can wrongfully presume that you can't be hurt and are careless with or ignore your feelings. Some see you as fearless; however, you do have fears of losing control or being removed from your position of leadership, strength, and power.

The Primary Spiritual Inhibitor That Blocks Your Frequency: Misplaced Desires

You have a tendency to be lured by unhealthy or misplaced desires. Your commitment to hard work can often lead you to a place of emotional and mental emptiness where temptation can grow strongest. Because of your intense resolve, you often won't notice that you are "on empty" until it is too late. You may decide to do something in a moment of weakness that causes a sense of shame, inhibiting your spiritual growth.

MEET SOMEONE WHO MAY HELP YOU

Karl Clauson. Karl is the author of *Thrill,*[1] founder of Lifelane180 Ministries, and the talk-show host of *LifeLane Live* at a Chicago-based radio station. Karl was the pastor of Change Point Church in Anchorage, Alaska, for ten years before starting Lifelane180.

*Most of our interviews have been with someone who shares the same personality as the chapter where their interview appears. Even though Karl is a "Joseph," he had some great things to say about the Samson personality type.

Tell us a little bit about your journey up until this point.

KARL. I didn't try to get into pastoring. I stumbled into it. Before pastoring Change Point, I didn't really believe the church could profess the kind of relevance we needed in the gospel. But eventually I was swayed. I spent nearly a decade in Alaska as the lead pastor at Change Point and it was quite a ride. At first, the church was named Grace Community Church, but we changed the name to Change Point. It really became that—a changing point for people. We saw life change happening on a regular basis. It became the norm. I remember moments when we had lines of people who had decided to follow Jesus, waiting to get what we called "new believer packets." Because of the church's growth, we brought on a considerably large amount of staff in a short amount of time with a variety of personalities and gift mixes, for sure.

What are you up to these days?

KARL. Lifelane180 has been quite a ride as well. We have stayed clear on our mission and vision to awaken a spiritual culture in the church that reaches the world. I believe that we cannot reach the world until we reach the church. As I have traveled around the nation to a handful of very significant churches, I have grown convicted and convinced that our churches are littered with lost people. They think they know Jesus, but they have an illusion of transformation. Lifelane180 exists to address that issue.

We speak at events in churches and have released a book called *Thrill* to get after this idea of really living the life God intended for each of us. Also, we are absolutely full steam ahead with getting the message on a radio show called *Life-lane Live*. Our hope is not only to put it into a large city but also to get it syndicated nationally.

From your perspective, what are some of the pitfalls of the Samson personality type?

KARL. One of the sticky points for this type of personality is their struggle to trust people enough to let things hang out there—the vulnerability factor. For Samsons, I think their resistance holds them back from authentic community and keeps people at arm's length. Usually, they have an underlying passion to be known, but there is a definite hesitancy to go there. Sometimes there has been an offense early on in their life, which caused them to feel burned. As a result, they remain guarded out of fear that they will get hurt.

What kind of advice do you give to people who are scared to be vulnerable?

KARL. I think a first step toward vulnerability would be to find a person who has a very proven track record. A proven track record not just in what they say, but also how they act. Do they talk about others positively? Do they keep confidential things private? Find valid reasons to call someone trustworthy. This will take some discernment on your part, but it is well worth it once you find someone you can trust. Once you find someone, you will likely start to find others, growing your circle of friends with whom you can be vulnerable. It is not necessary to bare all your emotions to just anybody—in fact, it could be dangerous. I think there is a better way to go. If you are careless about whom you choose to share your life with, you will likely get burned again, making you more seized up than before.

What advice would you give someone who has been hurt when he or she became vulnerable?

KARL. They need to embrace that pain fully. Because of the Samson personality type, the temptation is to just shake it off. In churches, we can sometimes do people a disservice when we try to fix them up too quickly. I have done this before with other people, and I can tell you that it is the wrong way to go. We need to allow people to feel the depth of their pain and deal with it in a healthy way. Pain is a mysterious grace of God that, for some reason, we often want to avoid at all cost.

Scripture is clear that we all should expect to get burned, betrayed, and backstabbed on this earth. It is part of what makes this world broken. So what do you do when it happens? If you try to get back on your feet, ignore it, and brush it off, you may miss one of the greatest gifts from God. You may find yourself becoming secretly bitter. Embrace the pain and you will find God at the bottom of your pain. That is why Jesus said, "Blessed are the poor in spirit, for theirs is the kingdom of heaven." When we feel hurt, He says, "Blessed are those who mourn." When we feel down, He says, "You are positioned for great things." I am absolutely convinced that the mysterious grace of God is often found in our pain. We need to be quicker to embrace it fully, because that is where great men and women are really born.

People with a Samson personality type usually have a great work ethic, but they can be seen as workaholics. What would you say to them in that respect?

KARL. Most people say, "Oh, you need to calm down" or "You need to read a book on why this pace is going to kill you" or "You need to be like that person who isn't as high-strung or driven." I think that is bad advice. God made Samson the way He wanted to make him. Is Samson bad or flawed? No. The question we should be asking is, "How do I channel the gifts that God has given me to serve Him best?"

There are misplaced desires and passions, for sure. But rather than trying to throttle back your passions or pretend they don't exist, do everything you can, by the grace and the power of God, to fall on your knees and ask for those desires to be channeled first and foremost into the deep, cultivating work of your relationship with God. If you find people saying to you, "Man, you are redlining it. You are pushing yourself over the edge here," listen to it, but be discerning with how you hear that input. Don't wish you had a different gift or a different wiring. Take it to the Lord and tell Him what is on your mind and heart. Say, "Lord, show me how to channel this thing. You show me where I am out of line. You show me how to throttle it down, if I need to." And then listen.

In those times, it would be wise to ask the circle of people you trust what they think. God will use them to speak truth to you. I heard someone once say that submitting your will to God is tough, but that's only 10 percent of the work. The other 90 percent is the obedience to His voice. It's when you ask, "What way are we going to go, God?" and then follow Him.

What are some recommendations for growth for people like Samson?

KARL. First, beware of your shell.

The reason many leaders are alone today is because they are still living with a shell of self-protection around them. Jesus says that if you want to live, you have to lose this life. I think the dilemma for any leader is the willingness to have the courage to fall to the ground and die—to lose this life. It is in our brokenness that God heals us. Salvation comes when we admit our dependence on Him and give up our shell of self-protection. It feels risky and vulnerable, but we must realize that our shell is a barrier to God's work in us.

Second, listen to God.

You will never be what God wants you to be if you compare yourself to others, especially to other leaders. Samson types might be perceived as "a little bit out there" sometimes, willing to do things other people aren't willing to do. Oftentimes, it is difficult to find good life examples to follow who fit the way you are wired. That is why Samsons must pay special attention to hearing God's vision for their life, not someone else's vision for their life. Spend time alone with God in a way that works for you. Study Scripture and gain as much wisdom as you can.

Do you have any final thoughts for us?

KARL. You are uniquely stamped, gifted, and called out by God. The temptation to fear perception needs to be shed. God has wired you for a mission and a future. He has given you a vision for something that may look quite confusing to others around you, but there is no need to worry. Find that time alone with God where He can fill you with the confidence and gifting He has given you. Build a few key relationships with trusted friends. You can hear from the Lord clearly and lock arms with people who believe in you in the same way God believes in you. Take hold of everything that God has in front of you and go for it!

KARL'S RESOURCE RECOMMENDATIONS

Willard, Dallas. *Divine Conspiracy*. New York: HarperOne, 1998.

Willard, Dallas. *Spirit of the Disciplines*. New York: Harper-Collins, 1988.

Nee, Watchman. *The Release of the Spirit*. New York: Christian Fellowship Publishers, 2000.

Foster, Richard. *Celebration of Discipline*. New York: Harper-Collins, 1998.

SOME THOUGHTS BEFORE MOVING ON

If you are like Samson, here are some suggestions for you:

- You are a direct communicator. In the process of expressing how you feel to those around you, be sure not to dismiss or invalidate the way they feel about the situation.

- You are independent with an inner strength and fighting spirit. Learn how to show the sensitive, softer side of your personality with people you trust.

- This month, invite one of your closest friends to dinner and then let him or her choose everything about the night. Learn to enjoy something you didn't decide on.

- This week, schedule a time to play your favorite competitive activity (tennis, chess, or whatever). Try playing the game for pure enjoyment instead of trying to win. Choose fun over victory.

Chapter 14

Jonathan

Casey Bankord

Jonathan was supportive, diplomatic, loyal, and discerning. He was relationally gifted and a committed friend. At one point, his father, King Saul, and his best friend, David, became vehement opponents. Jonathan sought to reconcile the two of them in a peaceful manner, but he had no success. He valued peace and healthy relationships so much that his father accused him of disloyalty. His desire for good, value of unity, and support of David were so strong that he chose to give up his right to become the king. And eventually, he gave up his life in battle for his father. David loved Jonathan and he committed to do whatever he could to protect Jonathan's family. Jonathan was self-sacrificing, almost to a fault, and put aside personal gain to maintain unity in his relational world.

ELEMENTS OF YOUR PERSONALITY

If you have a Jonathan personality, people feel accepted and at ease around you. You are not easily angered and you generally find a way to think the best about people and circumstances. Positive and kind, you naturally calm the waters when things get rough. People trust your objectivity and cool head. You have a natural way of diffusing tension and helping others consider alternatives. You are not stubborn and are able to reconsider your position, or at least let your position go, for the sake of harmony. Your greatest fear is that you will be disconnected from others; therefore, you work hard at removing obstacles to interpersonal unity. Alternatively, you can exhibit some avoidance behavior and can procrastinate, especially if there is a person or issue begging for unpleasant confrontation. You have always been drawn to spiritual things and you have a deep desire for a connection with God. You are non-judgmental, so people feel comfortable confiding in you. You are relaxed, know how to have a good time, and like to go with the flow of things.

The Best of You

You have a way about you that can ease hurts. Because you are easy to talk to and accepting, you make an excellent mediator. You have the ability to see both sides of an issue and facilitate others to get past their anger and put aside differences. Words that others might use to describe what they love about you include trusting, patient, unpretentious, good-natured, open-minded, and kind.

The Other Side of You

Although you are naturally a calming influence, you dislike conflict. You are often tempted to soothe rather than solve and avoid rather than confront. Many times this makes the conflict go underground and then come back later with a vengeance. It is important to remember that "peace faking" is not congruent with authentic, biblical community. When things get rough, you have a tendency to disengage and ignore real problems. However, ignoring your own problem is different from failing to rescue people who cannot help themselves.

The Primary Spiritual Inhibitor That Blocks Your Frequency: Inaction

You have a tendency to avoid conflict or tough conversations. You can become passive and be tempted to escape when there is or could be emotional pain. You are deeply burdened when there is relational unrest and have a hard time connecting with God until it is resolved. Often you will put off a confrontation for too long and then cause pain to other people by bringing an unnecessary level of intensity when you finally have the conversation. Bitterness and resentment can be dangerous pitfalls.

Meet Someone Like You

Casey Bankord. Casey is on the leadership team at Heartland Community Church in Rockford, Illinois, and serves as a worship leader there as well. He is a coauthor of this book and has played an instrumental role in the Monvee project since its inception.

What are you up to these days?

CASEY. My parents started Heartland Community Church in 1998 when I was thirteen years old. So I've gotten to see a local church grow exponentially during the last thirteen years, and I love what the church can accomplish in a community and in the lives of people. I've gotten to experience both the good things and hard things about a growing church.

I love being in ministry. I serve as a worship leader in a variety of environments at the church and I'm also on the directional leadership team. Monvee started at Heartland in 2006, so I've gotten to be a part of it in a variety of ways from the ground up. It has been so much fun and exhilarating to watch God work through ordinary people.

As a Jonathan, what stood out to you when you read your Discovery Summary?

CASEY. I definitely agree that my main issue is the avoidance of conflict resolution. I enjoy creating and maintaining peace. In social and work situations, I like to make sure people are getting along, understanding each other, and feeling valued. However, when things go wrong, people usually need to be confronted. I hate that. It weighs heavily on me when I know I have to do it. The very nature of conflict is disruptive, and I'd rather have peace. I've been taught over the years about the importance of resolving conflict in a healthy way, so I know I can't just avoid it or sweep it under the rug. But it's harder for me than I'm sure it is for other people. There have been times when I know I need to have a conversation and it is all that I can think about, which obviously has a negative impact on other areas of my life.

How does inaction in conflict become a barrier in your relationship with God?

CASEY. I've learned that focus is a very good thing. When we focus on any task, conversation, or goal, our chances of success increase dramatically. When I have an issue with someone that I haven't resolved with them, it's hard for me to lead worship, be attentive to my wife or friendships, or to pray. It tends to consume my thoughts, which I know isn't right. I find myself worried for no reason or preoccupied when I should be focused. Sometimes my wife will say, "Did you hear my question?" And I totally didn't. I was so tuned out thinking about the issue I have with someone (rehearsing what I will say and how I will say it) that I'm not even paying attention to the conversation I'm in. Not good.

I tend to do the same thing with God. When I'm consumed with the issue I have with another person, I hear Him less, I seek Him less, and I get wrapped up in my own internal conversation in my head. Since learning about my spiritual inhibitor, I've made it a habit to resolve conflict as soon as possible, so I can be free to listen to God and experience life fully.

What's an example of a time where you did not do this well?

CASEY. A few years ago, there was someone on our ministry team who was getting under my skin. I knew it, but chose not to address it. Eventually, that person began to bother other people as well, which exaggerated my feelings about this person. As the leader of the group, I knew I was the one who needed to address the person and talk through it. When that conversation happened, I brought way more energy than I was expecting and ended up doing more harm than good. I remember thinking, *What was that?* I had let my feelings go unchecked and they had developed into bitterness without me even knowing it. I ended up apologizing for my intensity, but the harm I caused left an indelible impact.

What is good about being a Jonathan?

CASEY. I love to mediate between people who are in a disagreement. Seeing both sides is easy for me. There are days where I resolve a conflict within the team I'm on and when

I go home, I tell my wife how much I love my job. I truly love it.

I like to listen to people's issues and help them see things they may not be seeing. I rarely get angry and tend to keep my cool. Because Jonathans are so bothered by conflict, we can't reach peace in our hearts until our relational world is clean, which propels us to approach it even if it is hard. Jonathans are pleasant to be around, but as I mentioned, they have to be careful not to conceal their bitterness.

What is a struggle for people like you?

CASEY. I care too much about what people think of me. When someone is mad at me, it really bothers me. I like it when people like me. Therefore, it's hard for me to ignore people's critical or negative words. I take them to heart and place a high value on them. I can get myself in a ditch based on what other people think of me. Knowing what God and people who are close to me think of me has become very important to my spiritual and emotional health.

What are some recommendations for personal growth for people like you?

CASEY. First, take an inventory.

Our teaching pastor, Mike Breaux, regularly challenges us to take a conscious inventory of what is going on inside our hearts and minds. Doing this has been critical for me. I need to ask myself, "Is there anyone that I need to resolve an issue with? Am I holding on to any bitterness that I need to release?" When I identify an issue, I commit to resolving it that week—not later.

Taking an inventory in other areas of my life has been helpful too. I try to pay attention to my health, my attitude, my workload, and my anxiety levels. Dallas Willard once said the best way to measure your spiritual and emotional health is to ask yourself two questions: "Am I becoming more or less irritable these days?" and, "Am I becoming more or less discouraged these days?"[1] Those two questions are helpful indicators of where we are placing our worth.

Second, natural is good.

Because Jonathans are so affected by what others think, they tend to listen to advice more intently. Sometimes when I process my issue with a mentor or friend, they coach me on how I should handle it. That works sometimes, and other times it doesn't. Recently, I took some advice from a friend and tried to approach an issue with someone in a way that felt really unnatural for me. It was awkward; I stumbled around and became more confusing, causing the issue to grow. Approach the person in the way that feels natural to you. God has gifted you with natural social intelligence, so lean into that strength. But remember to be bold. This is not an excuse to wimp out.

Courageously lean into your strengths and create peace in your relationships.

Finally, spend time with God.

I know this sounds simple—and it is. Spending dedicated, focused time alone with God is essential for our personality type. We need to be reminded about the truths that God promises in Scripture, and our foundation needs to be based in Him. If you don't spend enough time alone with God, people will shape you in unhealthy ways. Let God shape you when you are by yourself. Take a walk. Read a good book. Take a long drive. Spending time with God goes a long, long way to eliminating what inhibits your growth, growing every relationship you have, and allowing you to leverage your strengths to help people live in harmony with each other.

Do you have any final thoughts?

CASEY. Be useful with the way God made you. Be proactive about helping people deal with conflict. While you are doing that, be sure you are clean with others too. Most of the time, the issue is easy to resolve and peace is attainable. Stop worrying so much. God is good and people are generally good too. Trust in your ability to navigate tough conversations and go for it.

You feel things deeply. It's a gift. The downside is that you may feel overwhelmed and overburdened at times. Surround yourself with people who can communicate the truth to you and help you see things the way they really are. True, authentic friendships are priceless for you staying on track. Be persistent about finding good friends and cultivate those relationships with intensity.

Because you tend to be self-sacrificing, pay attention to your energy levels. Otherwise, you will compromise your own needs to the point of unnecessary pain. Remember that God has created you and loves you just the way you are. You don't need to prove yourself to be worthy of love. He loves you with a perfect, unending, unconditional love. Learn to lean into that truth.

Casey's Resource Recommendations

Tozer, A. W. *The Knowledge of the Holy.* New York: HarperOne, 1961.

Hybels, Bill. *Too Busy Not to Pray.* Downers Grove, IL: InterVarsity Press, 2008.

Scazzero, Peter. *Emotionally Healthy Spirituality.* Nashville: Thomas Nelson, 2006.

Foreman, Jon. *Spring.* Credential Records and lowercase people records, 2008. CD.

Batterson, Mark. *In a Pit with a Lion on a Snowy Day.* Colorado Springs: Multnomah, 2006.

SOME THOUGHTS BEFORE MOVING ON

If you are like Jonathan, here are some suggestions for you:

- Don't be afraid of conflict. The next time you are faced with a difficult situation, be courageous to be the first to work toward positive change. Matthew 18 is a great place to start when it's time for you to act.

- You are thought of as a great listener, but don't be afraid to bring up what is going on in your life. Your role in the relationship is not just to hear; it is equally important that you are heard.

- For the next week, set a specific time on specific days to do some focused spiritual-growth exercises. It isn't as important what you do; it's more important that you follow through completely on this as a goal. It is important that the goals you set have deadlines. Start small and build on it.

- Remember that you have what it takes. You are enough in God's eyes.

Afterword

The Monvee Story

The frequency concept started long before we wrote this book. Casey and I (Eric) began working together over nine years ago, serving high-school and college students in our local church—Heartland Community Church. Casey led worship and I taught every week. We were having a blast. We both had a heart for students who felt disenfranchised from the church and God and needed the "light switch" to be flipped on in their life. We sought to create those "aha" moments for them to reignite their faith. Through some providential relationships that had been built through the years, we were invited to speak and lead worship for several Christian schools. One trip, in particular, was foundational to the *Frequency*/Monvee story.

In the fall of 2006, we were invited to lead a spiritual emphasis retreat for a Christian school in Charlotte, North Carolina, where students were bused to a retreat center in the mountains to hang out, play team-building games, and attend two chapels a day. Like a lot of Christian schools (Casey and I both attended them), the students were tired of chapel. They had heard the same messages in a variety of ways through hundreds of chapels and had grown numb to the powerful stories in the Bible. Quite clearly, we had a challenge in front of us. However, through God's grace and power, the experience was incredible and transformational in the lives of those students. We watched hundreds of jaded, disenchanted high-school students realize the grace God showed them through Jesus. We watched hundreds of lives being affected and changed, leaving us inspired, fired up, and grateful for what God had done.

However, when we boarded the plane on our way back to Chicago, a pit formed in our stomachs. We began to ask, "What is next for those students? Where do they go and what do they do now that they have made a first-time decision or recommitment to follow Jesus?" We weren't the first youth pastors in the world to ever leave a retreat asking, "How do I help these kids continue what they experienced at this retreat?" It is the "great retreat challenge" that we all struggle to solve. Students have a desire, but rarely connect it with planned behavior that works for them and is sustainable. As a result, they drift back into complacency or indifference about God's role in their life. It's a frustrating dilemma. We asked, "How do we connect students with the right next steps (specific to each one) to help them continue to live life God's way?"

We started wondering, "If technology can match some-one up with the perfect movie, the perfect date, the right skin-care product, or the right used car, shouldn't it be able to match someone up with the right next steps for his or her spiritual growth, based on the uniqueness of each individual?" In essence, we were asking, "Why can't we use technology to help someone find and stay on their spiritual frequency?"

We landed in Chicago, went home to our families, let the question simmer in our spirits, and continued to discuss pos-sibilities. In the winter of 2006, Casey and I were part of a group of young leaders that the directional leader of Heart-land Community Church, Mark Bankord, put together to "get after" important initiatives in our church.

One particular meeting in February 2007 was pivotal to the eventual idea of Monvee. We were discussing the dilemma we felt with the students in Charlotte and were explaining how frustrating it was to know that they had no clear next steps for growth. As we discussed it further, Mark said that "the great retreat challenge" is actually "the great church challenge." At the time, Heartland had a growing number of people who felt stuck, plateaued, and bored with their relationship with God. It's easy to be offended by this, as pastors, or feel like you are doing a bad job; but we chose to take a deeper look into the source of the issue. We realized it had little to do with what we were doing. People in our church had heard fantastic teaching, experienced transformational worship, and learned principles through hands-on service to the less fortunate, but they still felt stuck. They would regularly ask, "How do I go deeper? What do I do next?" Mark tasked Casey and me with this problem and said, "Figure it out."

Casey and I, along with Mark Bankord and another friend, Jim Sheldon, began to sketch out the framework for what would eventually become known as Monvee. We didn't have extensive theological or technological experience or education. So our first step was to ask a lot of questions and experiment with our local church. Over sixteen hundred people signed up to participate in what we first called "A Different Way to Do My Life." They were all people who had a desire to go deeper and agreed to let us experiment with some ideas to help them. We created a box that had some short reading assignments, planning diagrams and tools, and a book and teaching series from John Ortberg. The box was marginally successful because people were still asking, "How is this specific to me?"

We poked and prodded this group of people with questions. The first obvious question was, "What has worked for you?" We made it a habit to regularly ask people what God had used in their life to grow them. Then we started thinking about the uniqueness of each individual and how that correlated with what God had used to impact each person's life. We needed some sort of spiritual/personality assessment to be able to recommend the right resources and activities to people for them to grow because we felt that a person's unique wiring should be an important component to the way he or she pursues God. We began to dream about a new kind of technology that could make the recommended spiritual-growth plan specific to each person on a deep level.

Through the assessment, we planned to identify the signature sin of each individual, as well as their personality, learning style, and pathway to God, and then recommend action steps for people that were specific to them, to be delivered through their local church. We met with Dr. Cornelius Plantinga, the head of the seminary at Calvin College at the time, and Dr. Robert Roberts, the head of ethics at Baylor University, to discuss our ideas and findings. We wanted to be sure we were on solid ground and not going to confuse people on their spiritual journey (and to be sure we weren't heretics). Along the way, other great minds of the faith such as Gary Moon, John Ortberg, Kent Hoskins, Mike Breaux, and Dallas Willard came alongside us to encourage, critique, and challenge our thinking. In summary, we got a thumbs-up from everyone and decided to pursue the idea further.

The next step was to explore technology. In the fall of 2007, we were introduced to some of the brightest minds in technology at ACS Technologies in Florence, South Carolina, to think through the technological side of the idea. Because of the time we'd spent with some bright theological minds mentioned earlier, we felt armed with a strong sense that we were onto something that would truly help people. We asked ACS, "Is it possible to build a tool that can measure someone's unique personality characteristics and then sort through all the spiritual resources available today in order to build a spiritual-growth plan?" The answer was, "Yes, you can. But not by yourself." This idea (and the execution of the idea) was much bigger than our current team could handle. ACS graciously took us under their wing, showed us the ropes of what we could and couldn't do with technology, and helped us assemble a team of people to accomplish this crazy idea.

Heartland Community Church is a church that is entrepreneurial at its core. The church started by using internal videotape teachings from Willow Creek as its teaching pastor on Sunday mornings before multi-site was popular. Actually, there was no such thing as multi-site when Heartland invented this concept. At the time, church experts assured the Heartland leadership team that there was absolutely no way that people would show up to watch their pastor on a screen. The founders felt strongly about their desire to bring the best possible teaching to their friends (who were drifting in their faith) in Rockford. A small twelve-person core started the church in the founders' living room. Despite regular feedback that this idea would not work, Heartland launched its first service in September 1998 in a local college auditorium with a VHS tape teaching from Bill Hybels and a worship set led by one guy on a keyboard. Thirteen years later, the church has grown and now has over six thousand people attending two campuses on a weekly basis.

Because of that culture of innovation, Heartland was a great place for the idea of Monvee to germinate and grow. However, once Monvee began to gain momentum on its own, the leadership team and elders of the church wisely chose to set Monvee aside as its own separate entity. Heartland was/is called to reach people in Rockford with the message of Jesus and Monvee had clearly grown to be an idea focused on the church across the nation as a whole. So Monvee became its own entity (not directly tied to Heartland) by becoming a company—a company, not a nonprofit organization. We knew that in order to deliver the long-term promise of a Monvee-type technology to ongoing users, it needed to be able to function independently of donor dollars. We began crafting a business plan that would make Monvee available to as many churches and individuals as possible at a fair price, sustaining the project in the long run.

Armed with a vision (and affirmation from theological and technological experts), Mark Bankord led the charge to tell our story, passion, and dream to potential financial investors. During that season, Mark and I flew all over the country to meet with potential investors who could fund this new idea. By early 2008, we had no takers on the funding opportunity. Most of the technology people we met operated outside the church segment and didn't understand why investing in an idea like Monvee made any sense from a venture-capital standpoint. We needed to find someone who was captivated by the vision and wanted to support the potential impact that Monvee could have on people's lives if it became a reality.

Then, we met Cliff Smith. Ironically, Cliff was from Rockford. We had flown all over the country meeting with dozens of people, but we eventually found our guy in Rockford, Illinois. Cliff wasn't involved in a church and didn't even describe himself as a follower of Jesus. However, there was something about the idea of Monvee and its potential to help people that resonated with Cliff. In February 2008, Cliff stepped up and seeded the dream. He saw the effect for good that could take place in peoples' lives and he said yes. Over the next six months, God brought other generous supporters alongside Cliff to help Monvee become a reality.

When we officially became a company, we got right to work. We met and collaborated with a design team based in California that came up with the name "Monvee," which is a loose translation for the Latin words for "one life" (plus, it was an available dot com domain). Then, we built a team that could develop the broad concepts that we had sketched out on whiteboards by turning it into a fully functioning technology that actually worked. It was a monstrous project. We made a decision early on to build a quality, smart tool and not just a fancy-looking one. For the first two years of the Monvee development schedule, we spent all our time and energy building the foundational algorithms that control the assessment and resource recommendation engine of Monvee.

Once that was completed, we began to build the "skin" of Monvee (the part of the technology you see when you take your assessment and build a plan). And eventually it worked. Someone could take an assessment; receive a Discovery Summary that outlined unique characteristics about them, identified the person's signature sin, and associated them with a biblical personality such as Jacob, Joseph, or Abraham; and then, through their local church, build a plan to grow based on that uniqueness.

In order to test the effectiveness of the technology, we needed help from churches and church leaders across the country. On October 7, 2008, we began a ninety-eight-day journey to travel 36,988 miles and sleep in twenty different hotels to accomplish the alpha phase of the Monvee development—a fancy name for "the first test." In the alpha phase, we had dozens of churches agree to have their leadership teams and key volunteers take the Monvee assessment that we had developed (a twenty-two-question, image-based test) and also take a paper-and-pencil assessment (720-question version from which Monvee was based). Once a particular group had taken both assessments, we compared the results. To our pleasant surprise, the Monvee assessment actually worked. Through the Monvee assessment, we could determine the personality, learning style, pathway to God, and spiritual inhibitor (the sin that is getting in the way of that person's spiritual growth) for any person, in 698 fewer questions than the written form! The churches that participated in the alpha phase gave us great feedback, ideas, and resources to recommend to other people who were wired like them. We are forever indebted to those one thousand volunteers.

Here are the names of some of the churches that helped:

- Southland Christian Church, Lexington, KY
- Saddleback Church, Lake Forest, CA
- Menlo Park Presbyterian Church, Menlo Park, CA
- Discovery Church, Orlando, FL
- Crossroads Community Church, Corona, CA
- Canyon Ridge Church, Las Vegas, NV
- Fellowship Bible Church, Little Rock, AR
- Heartland Community Church, Rockford, IL
- Christian Life Church, Orange Beach, AL
- Fellowship Bible—Brentwood, Brentwood, TN
- Faith Church, RCA, Dyer, IN
- Two Rivers Church, Lenoir City, TN
- Manchester Christian, Manchester, NH
- Real Life Church, Valencia, CA

- Christ Community, Greeley, CO
- Fellowship Evangelical Free of Knoxville, Knoxville, TN
- Constance Free Church, Andover, MN
- Five Oaks Community Church, Woodbury, MN
- Red Rocks Church, Golden, CO
- First Evangelical Free Church—Lincoln, Lincoln, NE
- Emmanuel Presbyterian Church, Thousand Oaks, CA
- The Ridge, New Berlin, WI
- Harbor of Hope, North Chelmsford, MA

Because Monvee was born out of a church and our whole team was actively involved in leadership roles in the local church, we wanted to deliver the tool to individuals through the local church. We agree with Bill Hybels, senior pastor of Willow Creek Community Church, when he says, "The local church is the hope of the world." When God's people are working together and thriving in their spiritual growth, amazing things happen as a result. We wanted to be a part of that. We believe that when individuals thrive in their relationship with God, they are able to contribute to the world, to the church, and to their family and friends in a way that they could not contribute before. We designed Monvee to be able to be customized by each church so that they could incorporate resources, classes, groups, serving opportunities, etc., that they were already doing into each individual's personal-growth plan. We also created a way for each church leader to see the aggregate reporting on the spiritual condition of their church as a whole (percentage breakdowns on personality styles, pathways to God, etc.). This information is priceless to church leaders when setting teaching direction, crafting short- and long-term strategy, and praying for the people they lead. All this new development needed another round of testing. So in 2009, we launched the beta phase of development—a fancy word for "the second test."

We had dozens of other pioneering churches step in to help out the Monvee project throughout 2009 as beta churches. These churches helped us continue to learn, ask the right questions, and rethink our approach. Like any new idea, we had to develop thick skin when it came to receiving feedback. People tore it to shreds at times, but we knew it would make it better, stronger, and more effective in the lives of people as a result. And for that, we were more than willing to endure the pain.

Along the way, we connected with John Ortberg, a well-known author and speaker who actually grew up in Rockford, Illinois. We had grown to know John through Heartland's relationship with Willow Creek when John was a teaching pastor at Willow. John's passion for discipleship, the spiritual flourishing of every life, and the potential of the church was contagious. We knew we needed to talk to him about this idea. When we did share it with him, he loved it and we clearly had a kindred hope for what could happen in the lives of people. We were blessed beyond belief when John decided to work with us on his recent book, *The Me I Want to Be*. As a part of the writing process, John came to Heartland to flesh out his content ideas for the book at a Saturday-morning workshop. We invited all the original people who had signed up for the first iteration of the Monvee idea at Heartland back in 2006. John collected feedback from that group of people, fleshed out his ideas, and wrote an incredible book about how we were all made to become "God's best version of ourselves." It was through *The Me I Want to Be* that people became aware of Monvee (the Monvee assessment was included in every book). When *The Me I Want to Be* released in January 2010, Monvee had its first users.

Over the next eight months, we began implementing it in more than three hundred churches across the country and continued to learn, stretch, and tweak the technology based on user feedback. In October 2010, we officially launched Monvee 1.0 (no longer in testing) and began planning for the book you are now reading.

We believe that God has given us an important mission to steward. God has wired each person uniquely, and there are a lot of people in the world who are stuck in their spiritual growth. Unfortunately, they lack the clarity that we believe we can bring with a tool like Monvee. No one should get a pass on growing spiritually. We believe that if we can help every person identify what is getting in the way of his or her spiritual growth, get it out of the way, and put that person on a path to thrive, we have done a very good thing for the church as a whole. From the beginning, we have tried to do whatever it took to see this project through and we will continue to do so. We hope you grow, your friends grow, and your churches grow. All for the glory of our *great* God!

Acknowledgments

From Eric

This book began to be written before we ever thought of putting words to paper. Over four years ago we had a crazy idea to create something new for people who really want to live like Jesus. In our wildest dreams, I could have never imagined where this little idea would take us. And along the way there have been many who on one level or another allowed us to chase this dream. First, to my wonderful wife, Chrissy. I want to thank you for trusting me, because most people thought we were both crazy! We both sacrificed time away from each other and you always extended me grace. You have been the best partner anyone could have hoped for. To my children, Daylie, Grae, and Harry, thank you for sharing Daddy for a season. You are my inspiration. To my mother and father, Jim and Joy Parks, thanks for all your support and belief in me throughout the years. I am who I am because of you.

To Mark Bankord, without your vision and relentless tenacity, Monvee would just be marker on a whiteboard—forgotten with so many other good ideas. You believed in this before anyone else could understand what God had given us. To John Ortberg, thanks for being a wonderful teacher to me; I admire you deeply. Thanks to the entire staff, leadership team, elders, and board of directors at Heartland Community Church for releasing me in my gifts. I'm eternally grateful. To Neil, Josh, and Trevor, your shared talents have helped turn our ragtag team into a well-oiled machine . . . most of the time. Matt and the development team, your work has been outstanding! Thanks for tirelessly making Monvee better. Nate, you have been in this from the beginning, and you have been a fountain of energy and a trusted friend. Corbyn, you make all I do better with your creativity. Thank you, Christina, for keeping me organized and on track; that is not an easy job! To Gregg and Andrea, thank you for your friendship; I am lucky to have you both in my life.

To Neil Plantinga, Bob Roberts, and Gary Moon, thanks for helping me shape my ideas and ground them in solid scholarship. To Dallas Willard, your words have been encouraging, your life . . . inspirational. To the Monvee team past and present, thanks for joining me in the adventure to help people grow in a way that is natural for them.

To all the early adopters, alpha and beta churches, and those that have adopted Monvee thus far, you are the pioneers that make innovation happen in the church. To Cliff, Brian and Bruce, Bob and Linda, Brandon, Randy, Stan, Harold, Peter, and Mike, thanks for investing in us.

To Dave, your have guided us masterfully and done it with humility. To Elizabeth Maring, you have been our great protector . . . thank you! To the team at ACS Technologies, you didn't have to believe, but you did and your support over the years has been priceless. Casey, we started ministry as partners and we do our best work together. This is one more example of that. Much love!

To Shawn, Chad, BZ, Todd, and Matt, I'm excited about what lies ahead. To Red Rocks Church, lives being radically changed in a creepy amusement park . . . go figure!

To the dreamers . . . don't give up. God is still in the business of the impossible.

From Casey

I swore I would never write a book until I was at least fifty years old. It still feels like I have so much to learn and experience in life. However, God gave us this opportunity and hopefully we have stewarded it well. I was able to be a part of the germination of Monvee and early phases of dreaming back in 2006 and 2007 and then rejoined the project in the last year. The real hard work was done by Eric, Mark, Dave, and the rest of the Monvee team. They have definitely lived out the adage to "leave it all out on the field." The amount of personal passion, commitment, and sacrifice I have watched each of them exemplify in the midst of both struggle and triumph (for the sake of this mission) is admirable, to say the least.

When it comes to writing this book, there are a lot of people to thank. To my wife, Kayla, you are the most beautiful person I know—inside and out. You have been patient with me with the workload of this project and your genuine support is remarkable. To my son, Wesley, thanks for waiting until four days after the manuscript due date to arrive in this world. Whew! Your daddy loves you with an indescribable love; I know how God feels about us now. To my parents, Mark and Sherri Bankord, you have done everything possible to release me to be a God-fearing, responsible, surrendered man and I will do my best to be that. I can honestly say that you did everything right as parents. Your love for the church and your love for each other are contagious, and I want my life to look like yours. To my other parents (in-laws), John and Sharon, thanks for your sincere adoption into your family and for watching (and loving on) Wesley when things got busy. To my family, Carson, Dustin, Ashley, Jon, Jonny, Chris, Christine, Collette, Sarah, and all the little ones, you are the best brothers, sisters, nephews, and niece a guy can ask for. To my friends Lonn, Kevin, David, Chris, Eric, Gregg, and so many more, you are more important to me than you may realize.

To Heartland leadership and staff, I was thirteen years old when you let me lead worship on the weekend for the first time. What were you thinking? Seriously, though, Heartland Community Church is where I have learned how to love Jesus, love people, and use my gifts for ministry. To say that I have been fully released in every capacity there would be an understatement. There is a palpable sense of God-fearing leadership in our church and I'm humbled to have all of you as an example. To the Heartland congregation, I'm so excited for God to work in and through us for years to come.

From Both of Us

To Josh, Trevor, Lonn, Kevin, Doug, Gordy, Kika, Jodi, Breaux, Debbie, David, Chris, Christina, Mark, Sherri, Kayla, Ashley, and many others, your revisions, feedback, ideas, and encouragement on this manuscript were a huge part of the formation of *Frequency*. This book would not have happened without you.

To Rob, Byron, Kris, Jeana, Sherrie, Morgan, and the rest of the team at Worthy Publishing, thanks for believing in us.

We both know that we were a shot in the dark for you, and we are very grateful that you let us write this book, supported us in the ways that you have, and have a similar passion to ignite spiritual growth in people.

To our editor, Jennifer, you are really smart and good at what you do. You have poured your wisdom into this book while letting the concept breathe.

To our interviewees, we are deeply grateful for your words of wisdom, friendship, and generous support of Monvee. We hope that people truly grasp the life learning that you shared in this book and take it to heart.

And finally to everyone who reads this book, thanks for joining the journey. Our intent is to help you put off what is getting in the way of your growth, but take it all with a grain of salt and ask the Holy Spirit to help you see the truth and thrive. We are still in the middle of trying to figure all this out and honor God with our lives as best we can. Our hope is that you are blessed and encouraged through this book to pursue Jesus like never before and that the collective fruit of our lives points people to Him.

Notes

Foreword

1. C. S. Lewis, *The Problem of Pain* (New York: Harper-Collins, 1940), 147.
2. C. S. Lewis, *A Year with C. S. Lewis* (New York: Harper-Collins, 2003), 393.

Chapter 1: You Have a Frequency

1. See, for example, Job 37:2; Isa. 21:7; 55:2.
2. Charles Spurgeon, "Pray without Ceasing," sermon delivered March 10, 1872, at Metropolitan Tabernacle, Newington, London, U.K.; available at http://www. spurgeon.org/sermons/1039.htm.
3. Frederick Buechner, *Wishful Thinking: A Seeker's ABC* (San Francisco: HarperSanFrancisco, 1993), 119.

4. Dallas Willard, video interview from the Monvee gathering, February 2009.
5. Marjorie J. Thompson, *Soul Feast* (Louisville, KY: Westminster John Knox, 2005), 9.
6. Leslie T. Lyall. *A Passion for the Impossible.* (London: OMF Books, 1965), 5.

Chapter 2: Finding Your Frequency

1. World Bank, World Development Indicators. www .data.worldbank.org
2. John Ortberg, *The Me I Want to Be* (Grand Rapids: Zondervan, 2010), 49.
3. Gary Thomas, *Sacred Pathways* (Grand Rapids: Zondervan, 2000), 14.
4. Malcolm Gladwell, "Malcolm Gladwell on Spaghetti Sauce," TED conference, February 2004; available at http://www.ted.com/talks/malcolm_gladwell_on_ spaghetti_sauce.html.
5. John Ortberg, from an informal interview in July 2011.
6. Gary Thomas, *Sacred Pathways* (Grand Rapids: Zondervan, 1996), Bill Hybels, *Courageous Leadership* (Grand Rapids: Zondervan, 2002), John Ortberg and Ruth Haley Barton, *An Ordinary Day with Jesus: Participant's Guide* (Barrington, IL: Willow Creek Association, 2001).

7. Learning styles from the Monvee Assessment.

8. Elizabeth Wagele and Renee Baron, *The Enneagram Made Easy* (New York. HarperOne, 1994). See also Richard Rohr, *The Enneagram: A Christian Perspective* (New York: Crossroad, 2001).

Chapter 3: Something Is in the Way

1. Rick Warren, *The Purpose Driven Life* (Grand Rapids: Zondervan, 2004).

2. Mike Breaux, *Identity Theft* (Grand Rapids: Zondervan, 2007).

3. C. S. Lewis, *The Great Divorce* (New York: HarperOne, 2001), 106.

4. Marcus Buckingham and Donald O. Clifton, *Now, Discover Your Strengths* (New York: Free Press, 2001), 148.

Chapter 4: Crafting a Plan

1. Dallas Willard, video interview from the Monvee gathering, February 2009.

2. William Paulsell, "Ways of Prayer: Designing a Personal Rule," *Weavings* 2, no. 5 (November–December 1987): 40.

3. A. W. Tozer, *The Knowledge of the Holy* (New York: HarperCollins, 1961), 1.

4. Dallas Willard, video interview from the Monvee gathering, February 2009.
5. Mihaly Csikszentmihalyi. *Flow: The Psychology of Optimal Experience* (New York: Harper Perennial Modern Classics, 2008), 48.
6. David Benner, *Surrender to Love* (Downers Grove: InterVarsity, 2003), 10.
7. Rick Warren, *What on Earth Am I Here For?* from *The Purpose Driven Life* (Grand Rapids: Zondervan, 2002, 2004), 5.

Chapter 6: Joseph

1. Pete Wilson, *Plan B* (Nashville: Thomas Nelson, 2009).

Chapter 9: David

1. Mike Breaux, *Identity Theft* (Grand Rapids: Zondervan, 2007); *Making Ripples* (Grand Rapids: Zondervan, 2006).

Chapter 10: Luke

1. Mark Batterson, *In a Pit with a Lion on a Snowy Day* (Colorado Springs: Multnomah, 2006); *Circle Maker* (Grand Rapids: Zondervan, 2011), *Primal* (Colorado Springs: Multnomah, 2009).

Chapter 11: Timothy

1. Jon Acuff, *Quitter* (Brentwood, TN: Lampo Press, 2011).

Chapter 12: Solomon

1. Shauna Niequist, *Cold Tangerines* (Grand Rapids: Zondervan, 2007); *Bittersweet* (Grand Rapids: Zondervan, 2010).

Chapter 13: Samson

1. Karl Clauson, *Thrill* (Grand Rapids: Credo House, 2010).

Chapter 14: Jonathan

1. Dallas Willard, quoted by John Ortberg at a Catalyst PreLab in 2010 in reference to a conversation he had with Dallas.

About the Authors

Eric Parks is the cofounder of Monvee and a part of the leadership team. He has been in ministry for nearly fifteen years and also serves on the leadership team of Red Rocks Church in Golden, Colorado. He has written and produced five film-based teaching series—the most recent: *Finding*. He lives in Littleton, Colorado, with his wife, Chrissy, and their three children, Daylie, Grae, and Harry. You can follow Eric on Twitter @ericparks or at his blog, www.ericparks.com.

Casey Bankord is on staff at Heartland Community Church in Rockford, Illinois as a worship leader and member of the directional leadership team. He is also an integral part of the team that birthed the idea of Monvee. He has been in full-time ministry since he was a senior in high school and is currently studying for an MBA in Social Enterprise at Northwestern University's Kellogg School of Management. He lives in Rockford, Illinois, with his wife, Kayla, and their son, Wesley. You can follow Casey on Twitter @caseybankord.

WORTHY
P U B L I S H I N G

IF YOU LIKED THIS BOOK . . .

- Tell your friends by going to: http://www.whatismyfrequency.com and clicking "LIKE"

  - Share the video book trailer by posting it on your Facebook page

  - Head over to our Facebook page, click "LIKE" and post a comment regarding what you enjoyed about the book

  - Tweet "I recommend reading #FrequencyBook by @monvee @Worthypub"

- Hashtag: #FrequencyBook

- Subscribe to our newsletter by going to http://worthy publishing.com/about/subscribe.php

WORTHY PUBLISHING
FACEBOOK PAGE

WORTHY PUBLISHING
WEBSITE